TEACHER'S PET PUBLICATIONS

PUZZLE PACK
for
The Midwife's Apprentice

based on the book by
Karen Cushman

Written by
Mary B. Collins

© 2005 Teacher's Pet Publications
All Rights Reserved

The materials in this packet are copyrighted
by Teacher's Pet Publications, Inc.

These pages may be duplicated by the purchaser
for use in the purchaser's own classroom.

Copying any of these materials and distributing them
for any other purpose is a violation of the copyright laws.

© 2005 Teacher's Pet Publications, Inc.
www.tpet.com

INTRODUCTION

If you already own the LitPlan for this title, this Puzzle Pack will refresh your Unit Resource Materials and Vocabulary Resource Materials sections plus give you additional materials you can substitute into the tests. If you do not already have a complete LitPlan, these pages will give you some supplemental materials to use with your own plan. There are two main groups of materials: one set for unit words (such as characters' names, symbols, places, etc.) and one set for vocabulary words associated with the book.

WORD LIST

There is a word list for both the unit words and the vocabulary words. These lists show you which words are being used in the materials and the clues or definitions being used for those words. You may want to give students a word list with clues/definitions to help them, or you may want students to only have a word list (without clues/definitions) if you want them to work a little harder. Both are available for duplication. The word lists can also be your "calling key" for the bingo games.

FILL IN THE BLANK AND MATCHING

There are 4 each of the fill in the blank and matching worksheets for both the unit and vocabulary words. These pages can be used either as extra worksheets for students or as objective parts of a unit test. They can be done individually if students need extra help or as a whole class activity to review the material covered.

MAGIC SQUARES

The magic squares not only reinforce the material covered but also work on reasoning and math skills. Many teachers have told us that their students really enjoy doing these!

WORD SEARCH PUZZLES

The word search words go in all directions, as indicated on your answer keys. Two of the word search puzzles have the clues listed rather than the words. This makes the puzzle a little more difficult, but it reinforces the material better. Two word search puzzles have words only for students who find the clue puzzles too difficult.

CROSSWORD PUZZLES

Both unit and vocabulary word sections have 4 crossword puzzles.

BINGO CARDS

There are 32 individual bingo cards for the unit words and 32 individual bingo cards for the vocabulary words. You can use your word list as a "call list," calling the words at random and marking them off of your list as you go, or you could use the flash cards by cutting them apart and drawing the words at random from a hat (or box or whatever). To make a better review, you might ask for the definition and spelling of each word as you call it out–or you could call out the definitions and have students tell you the words they need to look for on the puzzle.

JUGGLE LETTERS

The vocabulary juggle letter game is intended to help students learn the spellings of the words. One sheet has the definitions listed on it as an extra help for students who need it or to reinforce the definitions if you choose to do so.

FLASH CARDS

We've included a set of vocabulary flash cards you can duplicate, cut, and fold for your students. Some teachers make a few sets for general use by the class; others make a set for each student. Some teachers duplicate them for each student and have the students cut & fold their own. You can cut out just the words and put them in a hat, have each student pick out one word and write the definition and a sentence for that word. Students then swap words and papers, with the next student adding a sentence of his own under the last one. You can have students swap as many times as you like. Each time the student will read the sentences written prior to his own and then add a sentence. You can cut out the words and definitions separately and play "I Have; Who Has?" Each student in the room draws a word and definition. The first student says, "I have (the name of the word). Who has the definition?" The student with the definition reads it then says, "I have (the name of the vocabulary word she has). Who has the definition?" The round continues until all words and definitions have been given.

Midwife's Apprentice Word List

No.	Word	Clue/Definition
1.	ALYCE	Name for someone who looked like they could read
2.	ANKLE	It broke when Jane tripped over pig
3.	APPRENTICE	Assistant
4.	BAKER	Father of thirteen children
5.	BEETLE	Jane Sharp christened Brat this
6.	BOYS	Village ___ tormented Beetle
7.	BRAT	Knew no home and no mother
8.	BREAD	Gift from baker to Jane
9.	CAT	Beetle's only companion
10.	CHEESE	Newly named inn: The Cat and ___
11.	CLEAN	Word describing Jane Sharp's fingernails
12.	COMB	Beetle longed to own it: wood cat ___
13.	CUSHMAN	Author
14.	DEVIL	Left mysterious footprints
15.	DUNG	Warm, rotting muck: ___ heap
16.	EDWARD	Alyce sent him to the manor to do threshing
17.	EEL	Cat's rival in burlap sack in pond
18.	EMMA	Mother's whose baby Alyce failed to deliver: ___ Blunt
19.	ENCYCLOPEDIA	Magister Reese's book
20.	FAILED	What Alyce felt she did
21.	FIG	Best tasting food to Edward
22.	FLASKS	Beetle bartered for them at the fair
23.	FLOOR	Beetle's bed: cottage ___
24.	GAVE	Midwife's claim of what Alyce did: ___ up
25.	GREASE	Ointment for aching legs of mothers-to-be: goose ___
26.	GREED	Midwife's fault
27.	GROMMET	Smith's lardy daughter
28.	GUTS	Will says Alyce has these
29.	HERBS	Plants used to treat mothers
30.	HOOVES	Wooden prints carved by Alyce
31.	INN	Where Alyce fled
32.	JENNET	Innkeeper's wife: ___ Dark
33.	JOHN	Innkeeper: ___ Dark
34.	JUNO	Roman goddess of moon, women, and childbirth
35.	LITTLE	Baby that Alyce delivered: Alyce ___
36.	MANOR	Where Alyce sent Edward
37.	MIDWIFE	Woman who delivers babies
38.	MILLER	Threw things at Beetle for her incompetence: ___'s wife
39.	MURDERER	Water sold for remedy: ___'s wash
40.	NORTH	Where Beetle found Jane and the baker kissing: Old ___ Road
41.	NOTHING	Brat expected, dreamed, and hoped for this
42.	PLACE	Alyce's desire for her life: a ___ in this world
43.	PRETTY	How Will describes Alyce
44.	PROSPEROUS	Wife bore him a son delivered by Alyce at Inn: ___ man
45.	PURR	New name for cat
46.	READ	Alyce learned to do this from Magister Reese
47.	RED	Will Russet's hair color
48.	REESE	Writer staying at Inn: Magister ___
49.	RISK	Alyce feared taking this
50.	SHEEP	Animals Alyce helped to scrub
51.	SISTER	Manor folk thought Alyce was Edward's

Midwife's Apprentice Word List Continued

No.	Word	Clue/Definition
52.	SIX	Babies Midwife bore and lost
53.	SLAPPED	How Jane settled down miller's wife
54.	SWITHIN	Fair held at Goblet-Under-Green: Saint ___'s
55.	TANSY	Will's mother cow
56.	TWINS	Tansy delivered these
57.	TWO	Meals a day for Beetle
58.	WILL	Town boy Alyce saves
59.	WINDOWS	Beetle watched through these and learned trade

Midwife's Apprentice Fill In The Blanks 1

_____ 1. Beetle's bed: cottage ____
_____ 2. Midwife's claim of what Alyce did: ___ up
_____ 3. Town boy Alyce saves
_____ 4. Will says Alyce has these
_____ 5. Jane Sharp christened Brat this
_____ 6. Midwife's fault
_____ 7. Newly named inn: The Cat and ___
_____ 8. Knew no home and no mother
_____ 9. Best tasting food to Edward
_____ 10. Innkeeper's wife: ___ Dark
_____ 11. How Will describes Alyce
_____ 12. Assistant
_____ 13. Smith's lardy daughter
_____ 14. Babies Midwife bore and lost
_____ 15. Beetle bartered for them at the fair
_____ 16. It broke when Jane tripped over pig
_____ 17. Tansy delivered these
_____ 18. Cat's rival in burlap sack in pond
_____ 19. Father of thirteen children
_____ 20. Manor folk thought Alyce was Edward's

Midwife's Apprentice Fill In The Blanks 1 Answer Key

FLOOR	1. Beetle's bed: cottage ____
GAVE	2. Midwife's claim of what Alyce did: ___ up
WILL	3. Town boy Alyce saves
GUTS	4. Will says Alyce has these
BEETLE	5. Jane Sharp christened Brat this
GREED	6. Midwife's fault
CHEESE	7. Newly named inn: The Cat and ___
BRAT	8. Knew no home and no mother
FIG	9. Best tasting food to Edward
JENNET	10. Innkeeper's wife: ___ Dark
PRETTY	11. How Will describes Alyce
APPRENTICE	12. Assistant
GROMMET	13. Smith's lardy daughter
SIX	14. Babies Midwife bore and lost
FLASKS	15. Beetle bartered for them at the fair
ANKLE	16. It broke when Jane tripped over pig
TWINS	17. Tansy delivered these
EEL	18. Cat's rival in burlap sack in pond
BAKER	19. Father of thirteen children
SISTER	20. Manor folk thought Alyce was Edward's

Midwife's Apprentice Fill In The Blanks 2

_____   1. Wooden prints carved by Alyce

_____   2. Assistant

_____   3. Mother's whose baby Alyce failed to deliver: ___ Blunt

_____   4. Best tasting food to Edward

_____   5. Cat's rival in burlap sack in pond

_____   6. Magister Reese's book

_____   7. Woman who delivers babies

_____   8. Water sold for remedy: ___'s wash

_____   9. Writer staying at Inn: Magister ___

_____   10. Threw things at Beetle for her incompetence: ___'s wife

_____   11. Left mysterious footprints

_____   12. Will says Alyce has these

_____   13. Roman goddess of moon, women, and childbirth

_____   14. Midwife's claim of what Alyce did: ___ up

_____   15. Alyce learned to do this from Magister Reese

_____   16. Beetle bartered for them at the fair

_____   17. Fair held at Goblet-Under-Green: Saint ___'s

_____   18. Beetle watched through these and learned trade

_____   19. Where Alyce sent Edward

_____   20. What Alyce felt she did

Midwife's Apprentice Fill In The Blanks 2 Answer Key

HOOVES	1. Wooden prints carved by Alyce
APPRENTICE	2. Assistant
EMMA	3. Mother's whose baby Alyce failed to deliver: ___ Blunt
FIG	4. Best tasting food to Edward
EEL	5. Cat's rival in burlap sack in pond
ENCYCLOPEDIA	6. Magister Reese's book
MIDWIFE	7. Woman who delivers babies
MURDERER	8. Water sold for remedy: ___'s wash
REESE	9. Writer staying at Inn: Magister ___
MILLER	10. Threw things at Beetle for her incompetence: ___'s wife
DEVIL	11. Left mysterious footprints
GUTS	12. Will says Alyce has these
JUNO	13. Roman goddess of moon, women, and childbirth
GAVE	14. Midwife's claim of what Alyce did: ___ up
READ	15. Alyce learned to do this from Magister Reese
FLASKS	16. Beetle bartered for them at the fair
SWITHIN	17. Fair held at Goblet-Under-Green: Saint ___'s
WINDOWS	18. Beetle watched through these and learned trade
MANOR	19. Where Alyce sent Edward
FAILED	20. What Alyce felt she did

Midwife's Apprentice Fill In The Blanks 3

_____ 1. How Jane settled down miller's wife

_____ 2. Midwife's fault

_____ 3. Newly named inn: The Cat and ___

_____ 4. Beetle bartered for them at the fair

_____ 5. Where Alyce sent Edward

_____ 6. Threw things at Beetle for her incompetence: ___'s wife

_____ 7. Alyce learned to do this from Magister Reese

_____ 8. Alyce feared taking this

_____ 9. Brat expected, dreamed, and hoped for this

_____ 10. Best tasting food to Edward

_____ 11. Wooden prints carved by Alyce

_____ 12. Beetle watched through these and learned trade

_____ 13. Left mysterious footprints

_____ 14. Alyce sent him to the manor to do threshing

_____ 15. Town boy Alyce saves

_____ 16. Wife bore him a son delivered by Alyce at Inn: ___ man

_____ 17. Mother's whose baby Alyce failed to deliver: ___ Blunt

_____ 18. Gift from baker to Jane

_____ 19. Innkeeper's wife: ___ Dark

_____ 20. Tansy delivered these

Midwife's Apprentice Fill In The Blanks 3 Answer Key

SLAPPED	1. How Jane settled down miller's wife
GREED	2. Midwife's fault
CHEESE	3. Newly named inn: The Cat and ___
FLASKS	4. Beetle bartered for them at the fair
MANOR	5. Where Alyce sent Edward
MILLER	6. Threw things at Beetle for her incompetence: ___'s wife
READ	7. Alyce learned to do this from Magister Reese
RISK	8. Alyce feared taking this
NOTHING	9. Brat expected, dreamed, and hoped for this
FIG	10. Best tasting food to Edward
HOOVES	11. Wooden prints carved by Alyce
WINDOWS	12. Beetle watched through these and learned trade
DEVIL	13. Left mysterious footprints
EDWARD	14. Alyce sent him to the manor to do threshing
WILL	15. Town boy Alyce saves
PROSPEROUS	16. Wife bore him a son delivered by Alyce at Inn: ___ man
EMMA	17. Mother's whose baby Alyce failed to deliver: ___ Blunt
BREAD	18. Gift from baker to Jane
JENNET	19. Innkeeper's wife: ___ Dark
TWINS	20. Tansy delivered these

Midwife's Apprentice Fill In The Blanks 4

_____
_____
_____
_____
_____
_____
_____
_____
_____
_____
_____
_____
_____
_____
_____
_____
_____
_____
_____
_____

1. Warm, rotting muck: ___ heap
2. Where Alyce fled
3. Woman who delivers babies
4. Magister Reese's book
5. Wooden prints carved by Alyce
6. How Will describes Alyce
7. Midwife's claim of what Alyce did: ___ up
8. Roman goddess of moon, women, and childbirth
9. Water sold for remedy: ___'s wash
10. Will's mother cow
11. Alyce learned to do this from Magister Reese
12. Fair held at Goblet-Under-Green: Saint ___'s
13. Mother's whose baby Alyce failed to deliver: ___ Blunt
14. Gift from baker to Jane
15. Wife bore him a son delivered by Alyce at Inn: ___ man
16. Will Russet's hair color
17. Beetle's only companion
18. Alyce feared taking this
19. Writer staying at Inn: Magister ___
20. Manor folk thought Alyce was Edward's

Midwife's Apprentice Fill In The Blanks 4 Answer Key

DUNG	1. Warm, rotting muck: ___ heap
INN	2. Where Alyce fled
MIDWIFE	3. Woman who delivers babies
ENCYCLOPEDIA	4. Magister Reese's book
HOOVES	5. Wooden prints carved by Alyce
PRETTY	6. How Will describes Alyce
GAVE	7. Midwife's claim of what Alyce did: ___ up
JUNO	8. Roman goddess of moon, women, and childbirth
MURDERER	9. Water sold for remedy: ___'s wash
TANSY	10. Will's mother cow
READ	11. Alyce learned to do this from Magister Reese
SWITHIN	12. Fair held at Goblet-Under-Green: Saint ___'s
EMMA	13. Mother's whose baby Alyce failed to deliver: ___ Blunt
BREAD	14. Gift from baker to Jane
PROSPEROUS	15. Wife bore him a son delivered by Alyce at Inn: ___ man
RED	16. Will Russet's hair color
CAT	17. Beetle's only companion
RISK	18. Alyce feared taking this
REESE	19. Writer staying at Inn: Magister ___
SISTER	20. Manor folk thought Alyce was Edward's

Midwife's Apprentice Matching 1

___ 1. GUTS
___ 2. JUNO
___ 3. EEL
___ 4. MILLER
___ 5. MIDWIFE
___ 6. HERBS
___ 7. BREAD
___ 8. SWITHIN
___ 9. SIX
___ 10. COMB
___ 11. APPRENTICE
___ 12. CAT
___ 13. READ
___ 14. PLACE
___ 15. RED
___ 16. BRAT
___ 17. JENNET
___ 18. DUNG
___ 19. CHEESE
___ 20. GAVE
___ 21. FLOOR
___ 22. GREED
___ 23. EMMA
___ 24. PRETTY
___ 25. GROMMET

A. Fair held at Goblet-Under-Green: Saint ___'s
B. Midwife's fault
C. Beetle's only companion
D. Newly named inn: The Cat and ___
E. How Will describes Alyce
F. Smith's lardy daughter
G. Assistant
H. Will Russet's hair color
I. Knew no home and no mother
J. Midwife's claim of what Alyce did: ___ up
K. Innkeeper's wife: ___ Dark
L. Mother's whose baby Alyce failed to deliver: ___ Blunt
M. Woman who delivers babies
N. Babies Midwife bore and lost
O. Roman goddess of moon, women, and childbirth
P. Alyce's desire for her life: a ___ in this world
Q. Gift from baker to Jane
R. Will says Alyce has these
S. Beetle's bed: cottage ___
T. Beetle longed to own it: wood cat ___
U. Threw things at Beetle for her incompetence: ___'s wife
V. Plants used to treat mothers
W. Cat's rival in burlap sack in pond
X. Warm, rotting muck: ___ heap
Y. Alyce learned to do this from Magister Reese

Midwife's Apprentice Matching 1 Answer Key

R - 1. GUTS
O - 2. JUNO
W - 3. EEL
U - 4. MILLER
M - 5. MIDWIFE
V - 6. HERBS
Q - 7. BREAD
A - 8. SWITHIN
N - 9. SIX
T - 10. COMB
G - 11. APPRENTICE
C - 12. CAT
Y - 13. READ
P - 14. PLACE
H - 15. RED
I - 16. BRAT
K - 17. JENNET
X - 18. DUNG
D - 19. CHEESE
J - 20. GAVE
S - 21. FLOOR
B - 22. GREED
L - 23. EMMA
E - 24. PRETTY
F - 25. GROMMET

A. Fair held at Goblet-Under-Green: Saint ___'s
B. Midwife's fault
C. Beetle's only companion
D. Newly named inn: The Cat and ___
E. How Will describes Alyce
F. Smith's lardy daughter
G. Assistant
H. Will Russet's hair color
I. Knew no home and no mother
J. Midwife's claim of what Alyce did: ___ up
K. Innkeeper's wife: ___ Dark
L. Mother's whose baby Alyce failed to deliver: ___ Blunt
M. Woman who delivers babies
N. Babies Midwife bore and lost
O. Roman goddess of moon, women, and childbirth
P. Alyce's desire for her life: a ___ in this world
Q. Gift from baker to Jane
R. Will says Alyce has these
S. Beetle's bed: cottage ___
T. Beetle longed to own it: wood cat ___
U. Threw things at Beetle for her incompetence: ___'s wife
V. Plants used to treat mothers
W. Cat's rival in burlap sack in pond
X. Warm, rotting muck: ___ heap
Y. Alyce learned to do this from Magister Reese

Midwife's Apprentice Matching 2

___ 1. HOOVES   A. Water sold for remedy: ___'s wash
___ 2. READ   B. Baby that Alyce delivered: Alyce ___
___ 3. NORTH   C. Jane Sharp christened Brat this
___ 4. SLAPPED   D. Babies Midwife bore and lost
___ 5. JUNO   E. Plants used to treat mothers
___ 6. FIG   F. Town boy Alyce saves
___ 7. EEL   G. Fair held at Goblet-Under-Green: Saint ___'s
___ 8. INN   H. Meals a day for Beetle
___ 9. APPRENTICE   I. Where Alyce fled
___ 10. SWITHIN   J. Mother's whose baby Alyce failed to deliver: ___ Blunt
___ 11. BEETLE   K. Assistant
___ 12. WINDOWS   L. Cat's rival in burlap sack in pond
___ 13. LITTLE   M. Best tasting food to Edward
___ 14. SISTER   N. How Jane settled down miller's wife
___ 15. SIX   O. Alyce learned to do this from Magister Reese
___ 16. MURDERER   P. Manor folk thought Alyce was Edward's
___ 17. PURR   Q. Smith's lardy daughter
___ 18. EMMA   R. Beetle watched through these and learned trade
___ 19. BAKER   S. Roman goddess of moon, women, and childbirth
___ 20. GROMMET   T. Father of thirteen children
___ 21. FAILED   U. Woman who delivers babies
___ 22. TWO   V. What Alyce felt she did
___ 23. HERBS   W. Wooden prints carved by Alyce
___ 24. WILL   X. Where Beetle found Jane and the baker kissing: Old ___ Road
___ 25. MIDWIFE   Y. New name for cat

Midwife's Apprentice Matching 2 Answer Key

W - 1. HOOVES
O - 2. READ
X - 3. NORTH
N - 4. SLAPPED
S - 5. JUNO
M - 6. FIG
L - 7. EEL
I - 8. INN
K - 9. APPRENTICE
G -10. SWITHIN
C -11. BEETLE
R -12. WINDOWS
B -13. LITTLE
P -14. SISTER
D -15. SIX
A -16. MURDERER
Y -17. PURR
J -18. EMMA
T -19. BAKER
Q -20. GROMMET
V -21. FAILED
H -22. TWO
E -23. HERBS
F -24. WILL
U -25. MIDWIFE

A. Water sold for remedy: ___'s wash
B. Baby that Alyce delivered: Alyce ___
C. Jane Sharp christened Brat this
D. Babies Midwife bore and lost
E. Plants used to treat mothers
F. Town boy Alyce saves
G. Fair held at Goblet-Under-Green: Saint ___'s
H. Meals a day for Beetle
I. Where Alyce fled
J. Mother's whose baby Alyce failed to deliver: ___ Blunt
K. Assistant
L. Cat's rival in burlap sack in pond
M. Best tasting food to Edward
N. How Jane settled down miller's wife
O. Alyce learned to do this from Magister Reese
P. Manor folk thought Alyce was Edward's
Q. Smith's lardy daughter
R. Beetle watched through these and learned trade
S. Roman goddess of moon, women, and childbirth
T. Father of thirteen children
U. Woman who delivers babies
V. What Alyce felt she did
W. Wooden prints carved by Alyce
X. Where Beetle found Jane and the baker kissing: Old ___ Road
Y. New name for cat

Midwife's Apprentice Matching 3

___ 1. CUSHMAN
___ 2. EMMA
___ 3. JOHN
___ 4. BAKER
___ 5. MANOR
___ 6. BRAT
___ 7. JENNET
___ 8. CLEAN
___ 9. NOTHING
___ 10. NORTH
___ 11. ENCYCLOPEDIA
___ 12. SISTER
___ 13. READ
___ 14. DUNG
___ 15. COMB
___ 16. SLAPPED
___ 17. FAILED
___ 18. WINDOWS
___ 19. PRETTY
___ 20. PROSPEROUS
___ 21. ANKLE
___ 22. GREED
___ 23. LITTLE
___ 24. BOYS
___ 25. CAT

A. Alyce learned to do this from Magister Reese
B. Mother's whose baby Alyce failed to deliver: ___ Blunt
C. Beetle longed to own it: wood cat ___
D. Where Beetle found Jane and the baker kissing: Old ___ Road
E. Village ___ tormented Beetle
F. Where Alyce sent Edward
G. Beetle watched through these and learned trade
H. Magister Reese's book
I. How Jane settled down miller's wife
J. Innkeeper's wife: ___ Dark
K. Wife bore him a son delivered by Alyce at Inn: ___ man
L. Brat expected, dreamed, and hoped for this
M. Manor folk thought Alyce was Edward's
N. How Will describes Alyce
O. It broke when Jane tripped over pig
P. Author
Q. Knew no home and no mother
R. Father of thirteen children
S. Beetle's only companion
T. Warm, rotting muck: ___ heap
U. Baby that Alyce delivered: Alyce ___
V. What Alyce felt she did
W. Word describing Jane Sharp's fingernails
X. Midwife's fault
Y. Innkeeper: ___ Dark

Midwife's Apprentice Matching 3 Answer Key

P - 1. CUSHMAN
B - 2. EMMA
Y - 3. JOHN
R - 4. BAKER
F - 5. MANOR
Q - 6. BRAT
J - 7. JENNET
W - 8. CLEAN
L - 9. NOTHING
D - 10. NORTH
H - 11. ENCYCLOPEDIA
M - 12. SISTER
A - 13. READ
T - 14. DUNG
C - 15. COMB
I - 16. SLAPPED
V - 17. FAILED
G - 18. WINDOWS
N - 19. PRETTY
K - 20. PROSPEROUS
O - 21. ANKLE
X - 22. GREED
U - 23. LITTLE
E - 24. BOYS
S - 25. CAT

A. Alyce learned to do this from Magister Reese
B. Mother's whose baby Alyce failed to deliver: ___ Blunt
C. Beetle longed to own it: wood cat ___
D. Where Beetle found Jane and the baker kissing: Old ___ Road
E. Village ___ tormented Beetle
F. Where Alyce sent Edward
G. Beetle watched through these and learned trade
H. Magister Reese's book
I. How Jane settled down miller's wife
J. Innkeeper's wife: ___ Dark
K. Wife bore him a son delivered by Alyce at Inn: ___ man
L. Brat expected, dreamed, and hoped for this
M. Manor folk thought Alyce was Edward's
N. How Will describes Alyce
O. It broke when Jane tripped over pig
P. Author
Q. Knew no home and no mother
R. Father of thirteen children
S. Beetle's only companion
T. Warm, rotting muck: ___ heap
U. Baby that Alyce delivered: Alyce ___
V. What Alyce felt she did
W. Word describing Jane Sharp's fingernails
X. Midwife's fault
Y. Innkeeper: ___ Dark

Midwife's Apprentice Matching 4

___ 1. NOTHING   A. Assistant
___ 2. JENNET   B. Beetle watched through these and learned trade
___ 3. EMMA   C. Baby that Alyce delivered: Alyce ___
___ 4. WINDOWS   D. Knew no home and no mother
___ 5. WILL   E. Water sold for remedy: ___'s wash
___ 6. BEETLE   F. Jane Sharp christened Brat this
___ 7. MURDERER   G. Smith's lardy daughter
___ 8. APPRENTICE   H. It broke when Jane tripped over pig
___ 9. LITTLE   I. Town boy Alyce saves
___10. BRAT   J. Will says Alyce has these
___11. DEVIL   K. Fair held at Goblet-Under-Green: Saint ___'s
___12. TWO   L. Where Alyce fled
___13. SWITHIN   M. Roman goddess of moon, women, and childbirth
___14. TWINS   N. Brat expected, dreamed, and hoped for this
___15. EDWARD   O. Alyce sent him to the manor to do threshing
___16. GROMMET   P. Will Russet's hair color
___17. DUNG   Q. Village ___ tormented Beetle
___18. JUNO   R. Warm, rotting muck: ___ heap
___19. GREASE   S. Meals a day for Beetle
___20. INN   T. Left mysterious footprints
___21. ANKLE   U. Wife bore him a son delivered by Alyce at Inn: ___ man
___22. PROSPEROUS   V. Mother's whose baby Alyce failed to deliver: ___ Blunt
___23. GUTS   W. Ointment for aching legs of mothers-to-be: goose ___
___24. BOYS   X. Innkeeper's wife: ___ Dark
___25. RED   Y. Tansy delivered these

Midwife's Apprentice Matching 4 Answer Key

N - 1. NOTHING	A. Assistant
X - 2. JENNET	B. Beetle watched through these and learned trade
V - 3. EMMA	C. Baby that Alyce delivered: Alyce ___
B - 4. WINDOWS	D. Knew no home and no mother
I - 5. WILL	E. Water sold for remedy: ___'s wash
F - 6. BEETLE	F. Jane Sharp christened Brat this
E - 7. MURDERER	G. Smith's lardy daughter
A - 8. APPRENTICE	H. It broke when Jane tripped over pig
C - 9. LITTLE	I. Town boy Alyce saves
D - 10. BRAT	J. Will says Alyce has these
T - 11. DEVIL	K. Fair held at Goblet-Under-Green: Saint ___'s
S - 12. TWO	L. Where Alyce fled
K - 13. SWITHIN	M. Roman goddess of moon, women, and childbirth
Y - 14. TWINS	N. Brat expected, dreamed, and hoped for this
O - 15. EDWARD	O. Alyce sent him to the manor to do threshing
G - 16. GROMMET	P. Will Russet's hair color
R - 17. DUNG	Q. Village ___ tormented Beetle
M - 18. JUNO	R. Warm, rotting muck: ___ heap
W - 19. GREASE	S. Meals a day for Beetle
L - 20. INN	T. Left mysterious footprints
H - 21. ANKLE	U. Wife bore him a son delivered by Alyce at Inn: ___ man
U - 22. PROSPEROUS	V. Mother's whose baby Alyce failed to deliver: ___ Blunt
J - 23. GUTS	W. Ointment for aching legs of mothers-to-be: goose ___
Q - 24. BOYS	X. Innkeeper's wife: ___ Dark
P - 25. RED	Y. Tansy delivered these

Midwife's Apprentice Magic Squares 1

Match the definition with the vocabulary word. Put your answers in the magic squares below. When your answers are correct, all columns and rows will add to the same number.

A. APPRENTICE
B. BRAT
C. SISTER
D. FLASKS
E. BEETLE
F. REESE
G. CAT
H. EDWARD
I. PLACE
J. HERBS
K. DUNG
L. NOTHING
M. FLOOR
N. BAKER
O. ALYCE
P. MANOR

1. Assistant
2. Father of thirteen children
3. Plants used to treat mothers
4. Jane Sharp christened Brat this
5. Beetle's only companion
6. Brat expected, dreamed, and hoped for this
7. Where Alyce sent Edward
8. Manor folk thought Alyce was Edward's
9. Name for someone who looked like they could read
10. Beetle bartered for them at the fair
11. Alyce sent him to the manor to do threshing
12. Warm, rotting muck: ___ heap
13. Alyce's desire for her life: a ___ in this world
14. Writer staying at Inn: Magister ___
15. Knew no home and no mother
16. Beetle's bed: cottage ___

A=	B=	C=	D=
E=	F=	G=	H=
I=	J=	K=	L=
M=	N=	O=	P=

Midwife's Apprentice Magic Squares 1 Answer Key

Match the definition with the vocabulary word. Put your answers in the magic squares below. When your answers are correct, all columns and rows will add to the same number.

A. APPRENTICE
B. BRAT
C. SISTER
D. FLASKS
E. BEETLE
F. REESE
G. CAT
H. EDWARD
I. PLACE
J. HERBS
K. DUNG
L. NOTHING
M. FLOOR
N. BAKER
O. ALYCE
P. MANOR

1. Assistant
2. Father of thirteen children
3. Plants used to treat mothers
4. Jane Sharp christened Brat this
5. Beetle's only companion
6. Brat expected, dreamed, and hoped for this
7. Where Alyce sent Edward
8. Manor folk thought Alyce was Edward's
9. Name for someone who looked like they could read
10. Beetle bartered for them at the fair
11. Alyce sent him to the manor to do threshing
12. Warm, rotting muck: ___ heap
13. Alyce's desire for her life: a ___ in this world
14. Writer staying at Inn: Magister ___
15. Knew no home and no mother
16. Beetle's bed: cottage ___

A=1	B=15	C=8	D=10
E=4	F=14	G=5	H=11
I=13	J=3	K=12	L=6
M=16	N=2	O=9	P=7

Midwife's Apprentice Magic Squares 2

Match the definition with the vocabulary word. Put your answers in the magic squares below. When your answers are correct, all columns and rows will add to the same number.

A. WILL
B. BEETLE
C. RED
D. CUSHMAN
E. GROMMET
F. GUTS
G. NORTH
H. TWINS
I. MURDERER
J. CAT
K. APPRENTICE
L. LITTLE
M. INN
N. TANSY
O. DUNG
P. PURR

1. Warm, rotting muck: ___ heap
2. Beetle's only companion
3. Tansy delivered these
4. Town boy Alyce saves
5. Author
6. Smith's lardy daughter
7. Assistant
8. Will's mother cow
9. Will says Alyce has these
10. Will Russet's hair color
11. Where Alyce fled
12. Baby that Alyce delivered: Alyce ___
13. Water sold for remedy: ___'s wash
14. New name for cat
15. Jane Sharp christened Brat this
16. Where Beetle found Jane and the baker kissing: Old ___ Road

A=	B=	C=	D=
E=	F=	G=	H=
I=	J=	K=	L=
M=	N=	O=	P=

Midwife's Apprentice Magic Squares 2 Answer Key

Match the definition with the vocabulary word. Put your answers in the magic squares below. When your answers are correct, all columns and rows will add to the same number.

A. WILL
B. BEETLE
C. RED
D. CUSHMAN
E. GROMMET
F. GUTS
G. NORTH
H. TWINS
I. MURDERER
J. CAT
K. APPRENTICE
L. LITTLE
M. INN
N. TANSY
O. DUNG
P. PURR

1. Warm, rotting muck: ___ heap
2. Beetle's only companion
3. Tansy delivered these
4. Town boy Alyce saves
5. Author
6. Smith's lardy daughter
7. Assistant
8. Will's mother cow
9. Will says Alyce has these
10. Will Russet's hair color
11. Where Alyce fled
12. Baby that Alyce delivered: Alyce ___
13. Water sold for remedy: ___'s wash
14. New name for cat
15. Jane Sharp christened Brat this
16. Where Beetle found Jane and the baker kissing: Old ___ Road

A=4	B=15	C=10	D=5
E=6	F=9	G=16	H=3
I=13	J=2	K=7	L=12
M=11	N=8	O=1	P=14

Midwife's Apprentice Magic Squares 3

Match the definition with the vocabulary word. Put your answers in the magic squares below. When your answers are correct, all columns and rows will add to the same number.

A. JOHN
B. SHEEP
C. EMMA
D. BOYS
E. INN
F. GREASE
G. BEETLE
H. REESE
I. NORTH
J. RISK
K. HERBS
L. MILLER
M. BAKER
N. DUNG
O. TWINS
P. CHEESE

1. Father of thirteen children
2. Ointment for aching legs of mothers-to-be: goose ___
3. Writer staying at Inn: Magister ___
4. Tansy delivered these
5. Threw things at Beetle for her incompetence: ___'s wife
6. Mother's whose baby Alyce failed to deliver: ___ Blunt
7. Innkeeper: ___ Dark
8. Alyce feared taking this
9. Plants used to treat mothers
10. Village ___ tormented Beetle
11. Animals Alyce helped to scrub
12. Where Beetle found Jane and the baker kissing: Old ___ Road
13. Warm, rotting muck: ___ heap
14. Where Alyce fled
15. Jane Sharp christened Brat this
16. Newly named inn: The Cat and ___

A=	B=	C=	D=
E=	F=	G=	H=
I=	J=	K=	L=
M=	N=	O=	P=

Midwife's Apprentice Magic Squares 3 Answer Key

Match the definition with the vocabulary word. Put your answers in the magic squares below. When your answers are correct, all columns and rows will add to the same number.

A. JOHN
B. SHEEP
C. EMMA
D. BOYS
E. INN
F. GREASE
G. BEETLE
H. REESE
I. NORTH
J. RISK
K. HERBS
L. MILLER
M. BAKER
N. DUNG
O. TWINS
P. CHEESE

1. Father of thirteen children
2. Ointment for aching legs of mothers-to-be: goose ___
3. Writer staying at Inn: Magister ___
4. Tansy delivered these
5. Threw things at Beetle for her incompetence: ___'s wife
6. Mother's whose baby Alyce failed to deliver: ___ Blunt
7. Innkeeper: ___ Dark
8. Alyce feared taking this
9. Plants used to treat mothers
10. Village ___ tormented Beetle
11. Animals Alyce helped to scrub
12. Where Beetle found Jane and the baker kissing: Old ___ Road
13. Warm, rotting muck: ___ heap
14. Where Alyce fled
15. Jane Sharp christened Brat this
16. Newly named inn: The Cat and ___

A=7	B=11	C=6	D=10
E=14	F=2	G=15	H=3
I=12	J=8	K=9	L=5
M=1	N=13	O=4	P=16

Midwife's Apprentice Magic Squares 4

Match the definition with the vocabulary word. Put your answers in the magic squares below. When your answers are correct, all columns and rows will add to the same number.

A. NORTH
B. CUSHMAN
C. PLACE
D. ANKLE
E. NOTHING
F. EEL
G. BEETLE
H. SHEEP
I. CAT
J. EDWARD
K. MIDWIFE
L. PROSPEROUS
M. PURR
N. GUTS
O. RED
P. BOYS

1. Animals Alyce helped to scrub
2. New name for cat
3. Author
4. Woman who delivers babies
5. Alyce sent him to the manor to do threshing
6. Alyce's desire for her life: a ___ in this world
7. Village ___ tormented Beetle
8. Brat expected, dreamed, and hoped for this
9. Will Russet's hair color
10. Cat's rival in burlap sack in pond
11. Beetle's only companion
12. It broke when Jane tripped over pig
13. Where Beetle found Jane and the baker kissing: Old ___ Road
14. Wife bore him a son delivered by Alyce at Inn: ___ man
15. Jane Sharp christened Brat this
16. Will says Alyce has these

A=	B=	C=	D=
E=	F=	G=	H=
I=	J=	K=	L=
M=	N=	O=	P=

Midwife's Apprentice Magic Squares 4 Answer Key

Match the definition with the vocabulary word. Put your answers in the magic squares below. When your answers are correct, all columns and rows will add to the same number.

A. NORTH
B. CUSHMAN
C. PLACE
D. ANKLE
E. NOTHING
F. EEL
G. BEETLE
H. SHEEP
I. CAT
J. EDWARD
K. MIDWIFE
L. PROSPEROUS
M. PURR
N. GUTS
O. RED
P. BOYS

1. Animals Alyce helped to scrub
2. New name for cat
3. Author
4. Woman who delivers babies
5. Alyce sent him to the manor to do threshing
6. Alyce's desire for her life: a ___ in this world
7. Village ___ tormented Beetle
8. Brat expected, dreamed, and hoped for this
9. Will Russet's hair color
10. Cat's rival in burlap sack in pond
11. Beetle's only companion
12. It broke when Jane tripped over pig
13. Where Beetle found Jane and the baker kissing: Old ___ Road
14. Wife bore him a son delivered by Alyce at Inn: ___ man
15. Jane Sharp christened Brat this
16. Will says Alyce has these

A=13	B=3	C=6	D=12
E=8	F=10	G=15	H=1
I=11	J=5	K=4	L=14
M=2	N=16	O=9	P=7

Midwife's Apprentice Word Search 1

```
B Q N B E S E E H C H E R B S C A R
A Z I V E D W R Y M L I V E D U P F
K D H B E E V G U T S E X M D S P C
E Z T L M P T H Z K A H A H K H R Y
R A I D E P O L C Y C N E N H M E T
N A W L B A L A E F O S S E D A N Q
F N S P B L T A Y R Z N D Y P N T B
D G K G B S I G C S R I P U R R I S
C N S Y O B N F A E D W A R D E C B
M I A V M U N L L V E T M E Q E E N
T H L W D Y P L S O E L M R X S D C
N T F R E R I F L O R E E F E H W
J O H N E M S I X H E O B D W I L L
C N R T R A Z G Y L W M J R B N G N
W K T T G L D J K T O V Q U E R K F
Y Y B Q H J V N E C Y L A M N A A J
G R E A S E A S J E N N E T G O D T
```

Alyce feared taking this (4)
Alyce learned to do this from Magister Reese (4)
Alyce sent him to the manor to do threshing (6)
Alyce's desire for her life: a ___ in this world (5)
Animals Alyce helped to scrub (5)
Assistant (10)
Author (7)
Babies Midwife bore and lost (3)
Beetle bartered for them at the fair (6)
Beetle longed to own it: wood cat ___ (4)
Beetle's bed: cottage ____ (5)
Beetle's only companion (3)
Best tasting food to Edward (3)
Brat expected, dreamed, and hoped for this (7)
Cat's rival in burlap sack in pond (3)
Fair held at Goblet-Under-Green: Saint ___'s (7)
Father of thirteen children (5)
Gift from baker to Jane (5)
How Jane settled down miller's wife (7)
How Will describes Alyce (6)
Innkeeper's wife: ___ Dark (6)
Innkeeper: ___ Dark (4)
It broke when Jane tripped over pig (5)
Jane Sharp christened Brat this (6)
Knew no home and no mother (4)
Left mysterious footprints (5)
Magister Reese's book (12)
Meals a day for Beetle (3)

Midwife's claim of what Alyce did: ___ up (4)
Midwife's fault (5)
Mother's whose baby Alyce failed to deliver: ___ Blunt (4)
Name for someone who looked like they could read (5)
New name for cat (4)
Newly named inn: The Cat and ___ (6)
Ointment for aching legs of mothers-to-be: goose ___ (6)
Plants used to treat mothers (5)
Roman goddess of moon, women, and childbirth (4)
Tansy delivered these (5)
Threw things at Beetle for her incompetence: ___'s wife (6)
Town boy Alyce saves (4)
Village ___ tormented Beetle (4)
Warm, rotting muck: ___ heap (4)
Water sold for remedy: ___'s wash (8)
What Alyce felt she did (6)
Where Alyce fled (3)
Where Alyce sent Edward (5)
Where Beetle found Jane and the baker kissing: Old ___ Road (5)
Will Russet's hair color (3)
Will says Alyce has these (4)
Will's mother cow (5)
Wooden prints carved by Alyce (6)
Word describing Jane Sharp's fingernails (5)
Writer staying at Inn: Magister ___ (5)

Midwife's Apprentice Word Search 1 Answer Key

Alyce feared taking this (4)
Alyce learned to do this from Magister Reese (4)
Alyce sent him to the manor to do threshing (6)
Alyce's desire for her life: a ___ in this world (5)
Animals Alyce helped to scrub (5)
Assistant (10)
Author (7)
Babies Midwife bore and lost (3)
Beetle bartered for them at the fair (6)
Beetle longed to own it: wood cat ___ (4)
Beetle's bed: cottage ____ (5)
Beetle's only companion (3)
Best tasting food to Edward (3)
Brat expected, dreamed, and hoped for this (7)
Cat's rival in burlap sack in pond (3)
Fair held at Goblet-Under-Green: Saint ___'s (7)
Father of thirteen children (5)
Gift from baker to Jane (5)
How Jane settled down miller's wife (7)
How Will describes Alyce (6)
Innkeeper's wife: ___ Dark (6)
Innkeeper: ___ Dark (4)
It broke when Jane tripped over pig (5)
Jane Sharp christened Brat this (6)
Knew no home and no mother (4)
Left mysterious footprints (5)
Magister Reese's book (12)
Meals a day for Beetle (3)

Midwife's claim of what Alyce did: ___ up (4)
Midwife's fault (5)
Mother's whose baby Alyce failed to deliver: ___ Blunt (4)
Name for someone who looked like they could read (5)
New name for cat (4)
Newly named inn: The Cat and ___ (6)
Ointment for aching legs of mothers-to-be: goose ___ (6)
Plants used to treat mothers (5)
Roman goddess of moon, women, and childbirth (4)
Tansy delivered these (5)
Threw things at Beetle for her incompetence: ___'s wife (6)
Town boy Alyce saves (4)
Village ___ tormented Beetle (4)
Warm, rotting muck: ___ heap (4)
Water sold for remedy: ___'s wash (8)
What Alyce felt she did (6)
Where Alyce fled (3)
Where Alyce sent Edward (5)
Where Beetle found Jane and the baker kissing: Old ___ Road (5)
Will Russet's hair color (3)
Will says Alyce has these (4)
Will's mother cow (5)
Wooden prints carved by Alyce (6)
Word describing Jane Sharp's fingernails (5)
Writer staying at Inn: Magister ___ (5)

Midwife's Apprentice Word Search 2

```
P Q L T G F B N S F L A S K S K R R
R B M W R V R O N I H T I W S R O M
O N M O E Z E R Y G Z Z X I U O N G
S P Z Y E H A T R S B P R P L R A J
P M R P D C D H T W I N S F D E M Y
E C I E M I L L E R N S E D W A R D
R T X D T D J J C H E E S E C D F J
O N U J W T U E N W C V C O M B A J
U M T Q N I Y N B O T O S K B L I S
S E W G N T F N G R T O N M R R L D
G C W A L Y C E P E E H S B A K E R
B A E B T I S T L Y O B I M T V D D
L L V R R A N C S J H E M N I H P G
C P C E E L K N A W F E V L G E L Q
Y S E R Y C A Q G T I T R G U J E L
V S G J R T E L T T I L Z B T V L L
E X M U R D E R E R Q E L F S J H F
```

Alyce feared taking this (4)
Alyce learned to do this from Magister Reese (4)
Alyce sent him to the manor to do threshing (6)
Alyce's desire for her life: a ___ in this world (5)
Animals Alyce helped to scrub (5)
Babies Midwife bore and lost (3)
Baby that Alyce delivered: Alyce ___ (6)
Beetle bartered for them at the fair (6)
Beetle longed to own it: wood cat ___ (4)
Beetle's bed: cottage ___ (5)
Beetle's only companion (3)
Best tasting food to Edward (3)
Brat expected, dreamed, and hoped for this (7)
Cat's rival in burlap sack in pond (3)
Fair held at Goblet-Under-Green: Saint ___'s (7)
Father of thirteen children (5)
Gift from baker to Jane (5)
How Will describes Alyce (6)
Innkeeper's wife: ___ Dark (6)
Innkeeper: ___ Dark (4)
It broke when Jane tripped over pig (5)
Jane Sharp christened Brat this (6)
Knew no home and no mother (4)
Left mysterious footprints (5)
Meals a day for Beetle (3)
Midwife's claim of what Alyce did: ___ up (4)
Midwife's fault (5)
Mother's whose baby Alyce failed to deliver:

___ Blunt (4)
Name for someone who looked like they could read (5)
New name for cat (4)
Newly named inn: The Cat and ___ (6)
Ointment for aching legs of mothers-to-be: goose ___ (6)
Plants used to treat mothers (5)
Roman goddess of moon, women, and childbirth (4)
Tansy delivered these (5)
Threw things at Beetle for her incompetence: ___'s wife (6)
Town boy Alyce saves (4)
Village ___ tormented Beetle (4)
Warm, rotting muck: ___ heap (4)
Water sold for remedy: ___'s wash (8)
What Alyce felt she did (6)
Where Alyce fled (3)
Where Alyce sent Edward (5)
Where Beetle found Jane and the baker kissing: Old ___ Road (5)
Wife bore him a son delivered by Alyce at Inn: ___ man (10)
Will Russet's hair color (3)
Will says Alyce has these (4)
Will's mother cow (5)
Woman who delivers babies (7)
Wooden prints carved by Alyce (6)
Word describing Jane Sharp's fingernails (5)
Writer staying at Inn: Magister ___ (5)

Midwife's Apprentice Word Search 2 Answer Key

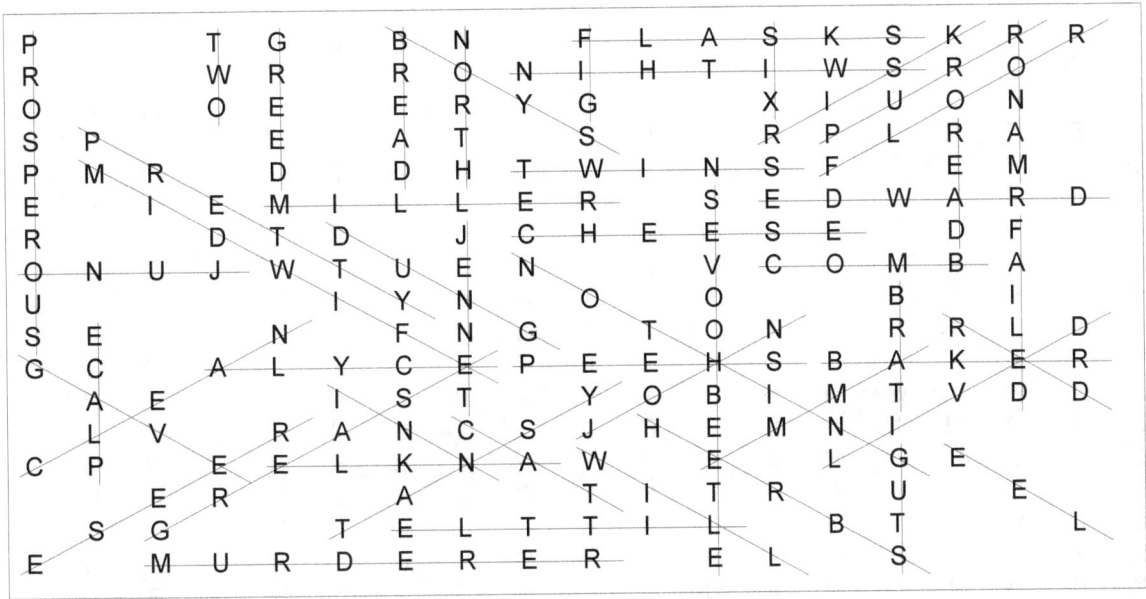

Alyce feared taking this (4)
Alyce learned to do this from Magister Reese (4)
Alyce sent him to the manor to do threshing (6)
Alyce's desire for her life: a ___ in this world (5)
Animals Alyce helped to scrub (5)
Babies Midwife bore and lost (3)
Baby that Alyce delivered: Alyce ___ (6)
Beetle bartered for them at the fair (6)
Beetle longed to own it: wood cat ___ (4)
Beetle's bed: cottage ___ (5)
Beetle's only companion (3)
Best tasting food to Edward (3)
Brat expected, dreamed, and hoped for this (7)
Cat's rival in burlap sack in pond (3)
Fair held at Goblet-Under-Green: Saint ___'s (7)
Father of thirteen children (5)
Gift from baker to Jane (5)
How Will describes Alyce (6)
Innkeeper's wife: ___ Dark (6)
Innkeeper: ___ Dark (4)
It broke when Jane tripped over pig (5)
Jane Sharp christened Brat this (6)
Knew no home and no mother (4)
Left mysterious footprints (5)
Meals a day for Beetle (3)
Midwife's claim of what Alyce did: ___ up (4)
Midwife's fault (5)
Mother's whose baby Alyce failed to deliver:

___ Blunt (4)
Name for someone who looked like they could read (5)
New name for cat (4)
Newly named inn: The Cat and ___ (6)
Ointment for aching legs of mothers-to-be: goose ___ (6)
Plants used to treat mothers (5)
Roman goddess of moon, women, and childbirth (4)
Tansy delivered these (5)
Threw things at Beetle for her incompetence: ___'s wife (6)
Town boy Alyce saves (4)
Village ___ tormented Beetle (4)
Warm, rotting muck: ___ heap (4)
Water sold for remedy: ___'s wash (8)
What Alyce felt she did (6)
Where Alyce fled (3)
Where Alyce sent Edward (5)
Where Beetle found Jane and the baker kissing: Old ___ Road (5)
Wife bore him a son delivered by Alyce at Inn: ___ man (10)
Will Russet's hair color (3)
Will says Alyce has these (4)
Will's mother cow (5)
Woman who delivers babies (7)
Wooden prints carved by Alyce (6)
Word describing Jane Sharp's fingernails (5)
Writer staying at Inn: Magister ___ (5)

Midwife's Apprentice Word Search 3

```
D U N G S Y O B G R O M M E T S B V
W D W U R T G C A C M J R A W I R Q
A K L T Z T Z R R K H I C D P X A G
M P T S Y E D F M W E R D N W E T F
U A P U R E T S N S L G N E I L O K
R N R W A P J N N D T T E C U N R E
D K N L E P L S R O T H E J H F L F
E L D S H N T A N W C C V R T Q E L
R E E W E N E I C S X O M I O W H N
R N R I B O N L C E X M L M N H O P
F Z C T S H N B T E R B X M G G O Y
S X Q H N I E E R D W G H R G L V P
Z J O S N J E O V S I B R E L I E R
N H T I G J F T N Q L F E P R V S D
G D E N A G Y L A S L A P X E D A H
R A V E E C V L M O O L B W D D D K
X T L M P S R S C O E J X T D E J
E C W P L P I F R H E Y R I S K R M
```

ALYCE   EDWARD   JOHN   REESE

ANKLE   EEL   JUNO   RISK

APPRENTICE   EMMA   LITTLE   SHEEP

BAKER   FIG   MANOR   SISTER

BEETLE   FLOOR   MIDWIFE   SIX

BOYS   GAVE   MILLER   SLAPPED

BRAT   GREASE   MURDERER   SWITHIN

BREAD   GREED   NORTH   TANSY

CAT   GROMMET   NOTHING   TWINS

CHEESE   GUTS   PLACE   TWO

CLEAN   HERBS   PRETTY   WILL

COMB   HOOVES   PURR   WINDOWS

DEVIL   INN   READ

DUNG   JENNET   RED

Copyrighted

Midwife's Apprentice Word Search 3 Answer Key

```
D U N G S Y O B G R O M M E T S B
          U   T         A   M     W I   R
A         T   T         K   I   D T X   A
M   P     S   E   D   M E   S   W I E   T
U   A   P U   R   E   S R   L   E N   N O
R   N   R W   A   T   N     L   E   J F
D   K   R     E   N   N     D   E   I T   E
E   L   W     H   N   D     O   E   R W   L
R   E   D     E   O   O     W       O     E
E   E         R   T   W     S       N     H
R         W   B   H   S     E             O
      J   I   N   I       E             L     O
  S   O   T   B   N     B R       G     I     V
    H O H N   H       E O       R R     V     E
    A N     N A     E E N     E E A     E     S
  G V E       G     C T A   S P P L         D
    E     E     L Y L M     N O D L
    C     P     R E E     O S B
  E M M A       G I F R   E Y R I S K R
```

ALYCE   EDWARD   JOHN   REESE

ANKLE   EEL   JUNO   RISK

APPRENTICE   EMMA   LITTLE   SHEEP

BAKER   FIG   MANOR   SISTER

BEETLE   FLOOR   MIDWIFE   SIX

BOYS   GAVE   MILLER   SLAPPED

BRAT   GREASE   MURDERER   SWITHIN

BREAD   GREED   NORTH   TANSY

CAT   GROMMET   NOTHING   TWINS

CHEESE   GUTS   PLACE   TWO

CLEAN   HERBS   PRETTY   WILL

COMB   HOOVES   PURR   WINDOWS

DEVIL   INN   READ

DUNG   JENNET   RED

Midwife's Apprentice Word Search 4

```
G P U R R C L E A N C B O Y S M V Y
U S I S T E R F G B O U A T F K T S
T Q Z B N C Y C R W Z R S K W I G X
S B S H F V Y O I O Z E T H E M S L
C T O N L J R C M N R F Z M R D S S
A J H K A P M L M D S I B R E A N Y
L Y T T S P M O E O P W P D C M D S
Y A K R K P R P T W G D X L U A N T
C O M B S B R E H S L I T H I N S C
E H F J L A S D T J S M T Z A O G G
N E E L Z C R I D T N P R E L R J Q
O D I E Q R A E E D Y P E A L E X X
T W O R S H E E P V E L A D R S N X
H A G O E E L G P I V A B E E E N H
I R D V J L R A I G C E B E N I P P
N D X L O I E L L G E M E L N S K C
G Y Z F N M S E Q Y I R A F E K Q M
S W D H M U R D E R E R S F A H L D
X
```

ALYCE	FIG	NORTH
ANKLE	FLASKS	NOTHING
BAKER	FLOOR	PLACE
BEETLE	GAVE	PRETTY
BOYS	GREASE	PURR
BRAT	GREED	READ
BREAD	GROMMET	RED
CAT	GUTS	REESE
CHEESE	HERBS	RISK
CLEAN	HOOVES	SHEEP
COMB	INN	SISTER
CUSHMAN	JENNET	SIX
DEVIL	JOHN	SLAPPED
DUNG	JUNO	SWITHIN
EDWARD	LITTLE	TANSY
EEL	MANOR	TWINS
EMMA	MIDWIFE	TWO
ENCYCLOPEDIA	MILLER	WILL
FAILED	MURDERER	WINDOWS

Midwife's Apprentice Word Search 4 Answer Key

ALYCE	FIG	NORTH
ANKLE	FLASKS	NOTHING
BAKER	FLOOR	PLACE
BEETLE	GAVE	PRETTY
BOYS	GREASE	PURR
BRAT	GREED	READ
BREAD	GROMMET	RED
CAT	GUTS	REESE
CHEESE	HERBS	RISK
CLEAN	HOOVES	SHEEP
COMB	INN	SISTER
CUSHMAN	JENNET	SIX
DEVIL	JOHN	SLAPPED
DUNG	JUNO	SWITHIN
EDWARD	LITTLE	TANSY
EEL	MANOR	TWINS
EMMA	MIDWIFE	TWO
ENCYCLOPEDIA	MILLER	WILL
FAILED	MURDERER	WINDOWS

Midwife's Apprentice Crossword 1

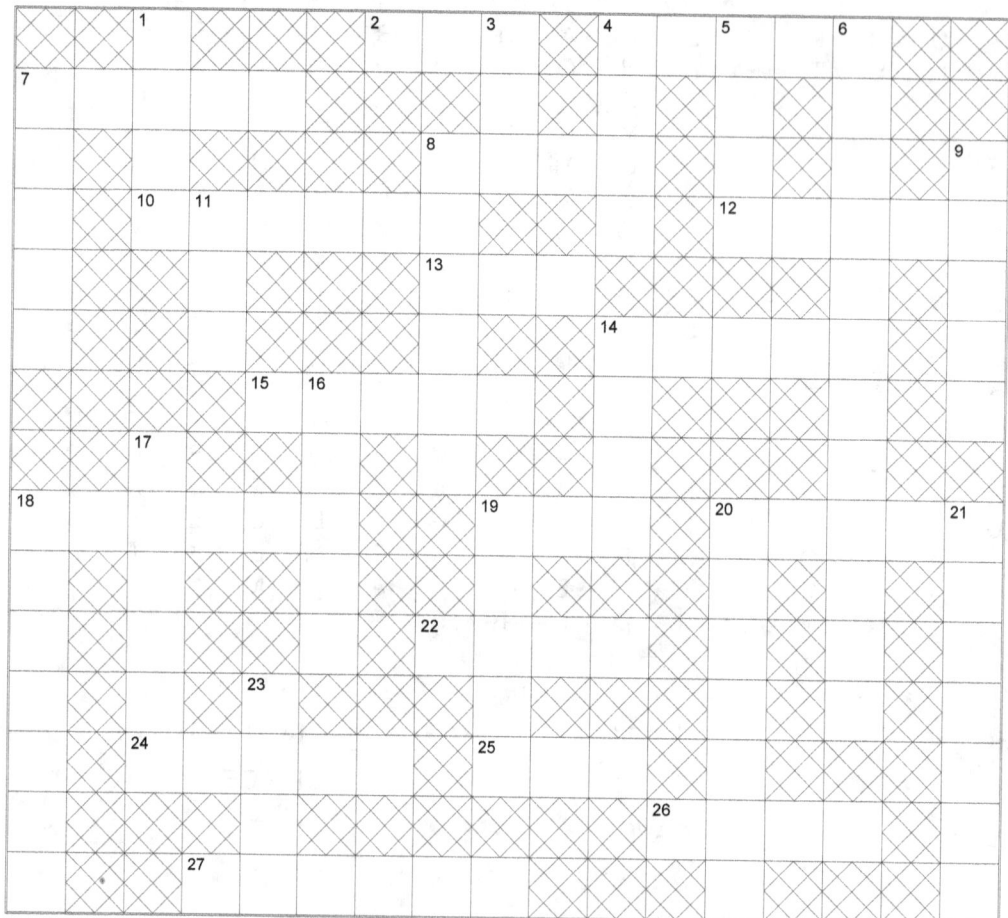

Across
2. Beetle's only companion
4. Writer staying at Inn: Magister ___
7. Tansy delivered these
8. Village ___ tormented Beetle
10. Baby that Alyce delivered: Alyce ___
12. Name for someone who looked like they could read
13. Cat's rival in burlap sack in pond
14. Left mysterious footprints
15. It broke when Jane tripped over pig
18. Threw things at Beetle for her incompetence: ___'s wife
19. Best tasting food to Edward
20. Word describing Jane Sharp's fingernails
22. Innkeeper: ___ Dark
24. Animals Alyce helped to scrub
25. Will Russet's hair color
26. Midwife's claim of what Alyce did: ___ up
27. Alyce sent him to the manor to do threshing

Down
1. Town boy Alyce saves
3. Meals a day for Beetle
4. Alyce feared taking this
5. Mother's whose baby Alyce failed to deliver: ___ Blunt
6. Magister Reese's book
7. Will's mother cow
8. Jane Sharp christened Brat this
9. Plants used to treat mothers
11. Where Alyce fled
14. Warm, rotting muck: ___ heap
16. Where Beetle found Jane and the baker kissing: Old ___ Road
17. Beetle bartered for them at the fair
18. Woman who delivers babies
19. Beetle's bed: cottage ___
20. Author
21. Brat expected, dreamed, and hoped for this
23. Alyce learned to do this from Magister Reese

Midwife's Apprentice Crossword 1 Answer Key

	1 W			2 C	A	3 T		4 R	5 E	6 E	S	E	
7 T	W	I	N	S				W	I	M		N	
A						8 B	O	Y	S	M		C	9 H
N	10 L	11 I	T	T	L	E		K	12 A	L	Y	C	E
S		N				13 E	E	L		C		R	
Y		N				T		14 D	E	V	I	L	B
			15 A	16 N	K	L	E		U			O	S
	17 F			O		E			N			P	
18 M	I	L	L	E	R		19 F	I	G	20 C	L	E	21 N
I		A		T			L			U		D	O
D		S		H		22 J	O	H	N	S		I	T
W		K		23 R		O				H		A	H
I	24 S	H	E	E	P	25 R	E	D		M			I
F				A					26 G	A	V	E	N
E	27 E	D	W	A	R	D				N			G

Across
2. Beetle's only companion
4. Writer staying at Inn: Magister ___
7. Tansy delivered these
8. Village ___ tormented Beetle
10. Baby that Alyce delivered: Alyce ___
12. Name for someone who looked like they could read
13. Cat's rival in burlap sack in pond
14. Left mysterious footprints
15. It broke when Jane tripped over pig
18. Threw things at Beetle for her incompetence: ___'s wife
19. Best tasting food to Edward
20. Word describing Jane Sharp's fingernails
22. Innkeeper: ___ Dark
24. Animals Alyce helped to scrub
25. Will Russet's hair color
26. Midwife's claim of what Alyce did: ___ up
27. Alyce sent him to the manor to do threshing

Down
1. Town boy Alyce saves
3. Meals a day for Beetle
4. Alyce feared taking this
5. Mother's whose baby Alyce failed to deliver: ___ Blunt
6. Magister Reese's book
7. Will's mother cow
8. Jane Sharp christened Brat this
9. Plants used to treat mothers
11. Where Alyce fled
14. Warm, rotting muck: ___ heap
16. Where Beetle found Jane and the baker kissing: Old ___ Road
17. Beetle bartered for them at the fair
18. Woman who delivers babies
19. Beetle's bed: cottage ____
20. Author
21. Brat expected, dreamed, and hoped for this
23. Alyce learned to do this from Magister Reese

Midwife's Apprentice Crossword 2

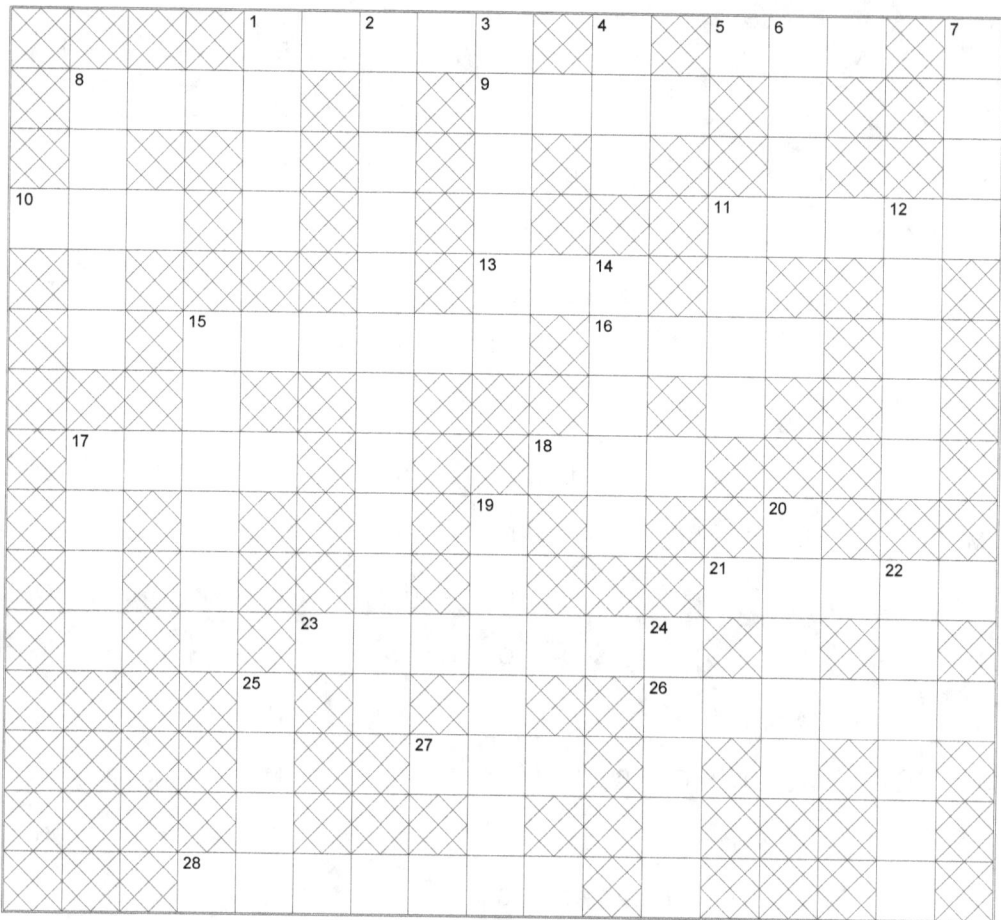

Across
1. Writer staying at Inn: Magister ___
5. Meals a day for Beetle
8. Midwife's claim of what Alyce did: ___ up
9. Warm, rotting muck: ___ heap
10. Cat's rival in burlap sack in pond
11. Word describing Jane Sharp's fingernails
13. Will Russet's hair color
15. What Alyce felt she did
16. Mother's whose baby Alyce failed to deliver: ___ Blunt
17. Knew no home and no mother
18. Best tasting food to Edward
21. Alyce's desire for her life: a ___ in this world
23. Beetle watched through these and learned trade
26. Wooden prints carved by Alyce
27. Babies Midwife bore and lost
28. Smith's lardy daughter

Down
1. Alyce learned to do this from Magister Reese
2. Magister Reese's book
3. Alyce sent him to the manor to do threshing
4. Where Alyce fled
6. Town boy Alyce saves
7. Innkeeper: ___ Dark
8. Midwife's fault
11. Beetle longed to own it: wood cat ___
12. Name for someone who looked like they could read
14. Left mysterious footprints
15. Beetle bartered for them at the fair
17. Village ___ tormented Beetle
19. Woman who delivers babies
20. Beetle's bed: cottage ___
22. Newly named inn: The Cat and ___
24. Animals Alyce helped to scrub
25. New name for cat

Midwife's Apprentice Crossword 2 Answer Key

			1 R	2 E	3 S	4 E		5 T	6 W	O	7 J
	8 G	A	V	E	N	9 D	U	N	G		O
		R		A		C		W	N		L	H

(Completed grid as shown)

R E E S E / I / T W O / J
G A V E N / D U N G / I / O
R / A / C / W N / L / H
10 E E L / D / Y / A / 11 C L 12 E A N
E / C / 13 R 14 E D / O / L
15 D / F A I L E D / 16 E M M A / Y
L / O / V / B / C
17 B R A T / P / 18 F I G / E
O / S / E / 19 M L / 20 F
Y / K / D / I / 21 P L A 22 C E
S S / 23 W I N D O W 24 S / O / H
25 P A W / 26 H O O V E S
U / 27 S I X / E / R / E
R / F / E / S
28 G R O M M E T / P / E

Across
1. Writer staying at Inn: Magister ___
5. Meals a day for Beetle
8. Midwife's claim of what Alyce did: ___ up
9. Warm, rotting muck: ___ heap
10. Cat's rival in burlap sack in pond
11. Word describing Jane Sharp's fingernails
13. Will Russet's hair color
15. What Alyce felt she did
16. Mother's whose baby Alyce failed to deliver: ___ Blunt
17. Knew no home and no mother
18. Best tasting food to Edward
21. Alyce's desire for her life: a ___ in this world
23. Beetle watched through these and learned trade
26. Wooden prints carved by Alyce
27. Babies Midwife bore and lost
28. Smith's lardy daughter

Down
1. Alyce learned to do this from Magister Reese
2. Magister Reese's book
3. Alyce sent him to the manor to do threshing
4. Where Alyce fled
6. Town boy Alyce saves
7. Innkeeper: ___ Dark
8. Midwife's fault
11. Beetle longed to own it: wood cat ___
12. Name for someone who looked like they could read
14. Left mysterious footprints
15. Beetle bartered for them at the fair
17. Village ___ tormented Beetle
19. Woman who delivers babies
20. Beetle's bed: cottage ___
22. Newly named inn: The Cat and ___
24. Animals Alyce helped to scrub
25. New name for cat

Midwife's Apprentice Crossword 3

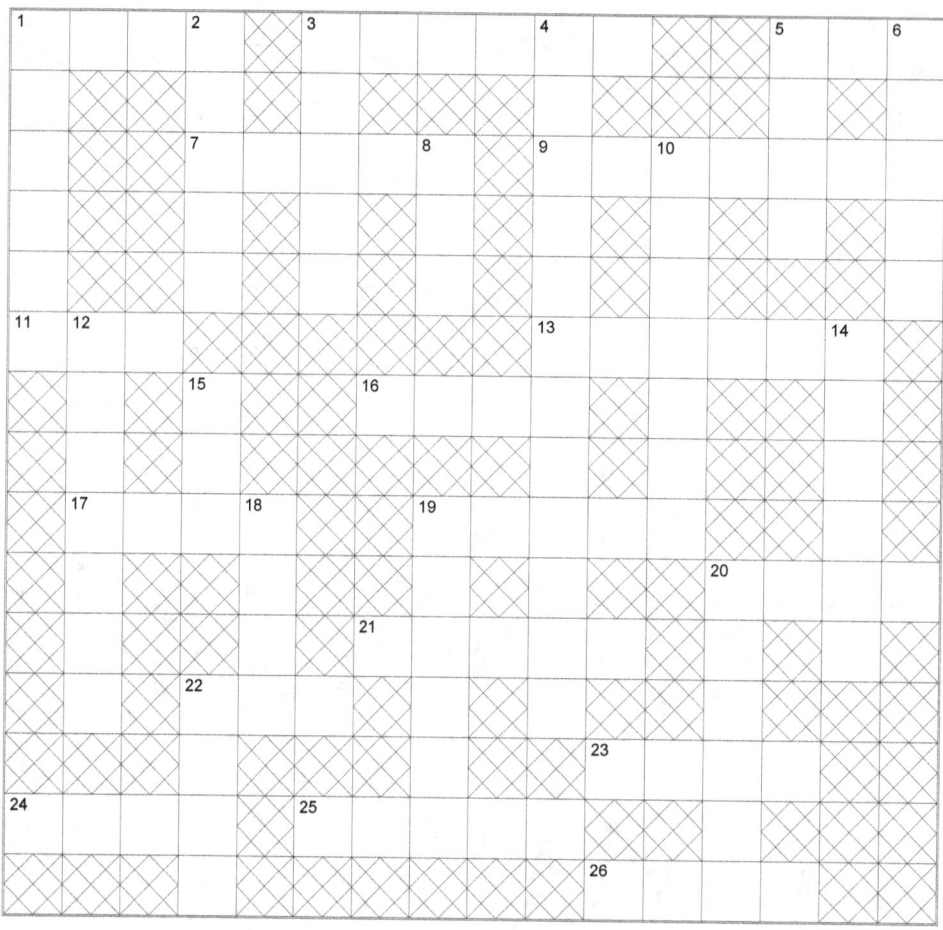

Across
1. Innkeeper: ___ Dark
3. Manor folk thought Alyce was Edward's
5. Beetle's only companion
7. Writer staying at Inn: Magister ___
9. Author
11. Meals a day for Beetle
13. Baby that Alyce delivered: Alyce ___
16. Roman goddess of moon, women, and childbirth
17. Warm, rotting muck: ___ heap
19. Word describing Jane Sharp's fingernails
20. New name for cat
21. Left mysterious footprints
22. Will Russet's hair color
23. Will says Alyce has these
24. Mother's whose baby Alyce failed to deliver: ___ Blunt
25. Midwife's fault
26. Village ___ tormented Beetle

Down
1. Innkeeper's wife: ___ Dark
2. Where Beetle found Jane and the baker kissing: Old ___ Road
3. Animals Alyce helped to scrub
4. Magister Reese's book
5. Beetle longed to own it: wood cat ___
6. Will's mother cow
8. Cat's rival in burlap sack in pond
10. Fair held at Goblet-Under-Green: Saint ___'s
12. Beetle watched through these and learned trade
14. Alyce sent him to the manor to do threshing
15. Where Alyce fled
18. Midwife's claim of what Alyce did: ___ up
19. Newly named inn: The Cat and ___
20. How Will describes Alyce
22. Alyce learned to do this from Magister Reese

Midwife's Apprentice Crossword 3 Answer Key

	1 J	O	H	2 N		3 S	I	S	T	4 E	R		5 C	A	6 T
	E			O		H				N			O		A
	N		7 R	E	E	S	E		8 E	9 C	U	10 S	H	M	A	N
	N			T		E			E	Y		W		B		S
	E			H		P			L	C		I				Y
11 T	12 W	O			15 I		16 J	U	N	13 L	I	T	T	14 L	E
	I				I		16 J	U	N	O		H		D	
	N			17 D	N	18 G		19 C	L	P	A	N		W	
	17 D	U	N	G		A		19 C	L	E	A	N		20 P	U	R	R
	O					V		H		D				U		D
	W					22 R	E	21 D	E	V	I	L		R	
	S					E			S		A			23 G	U	T	S
24 E	M	M	A		25 G	R	E	E	D			T	
			D							26 B	O	Y	S

Across
1. Innkeeper: ___ Dark
3. Manor folk thought Alyce was Edward's
5. Beetle's only companion
7. Writer staying at Inn: Magister ___
9. Author
11. Meals a day for Beetle
13. Baby that Alyce delivered: Alyce ___
16. Roman goddess of moon, women, and childbirth
17. Warm, rotting muck: ___ heap
19. Word describing Jane Sharp's fingernails
20. New name for cat
21. Left mysterious footprints
22. Will Russet's hair color
23. Will says Alyce has these
24. Mother's whose baby Alyce failed to deliver: ___ Blunt
25. Midwife's fault
26. Village ___ tormented Beetle

Down
1. Innkeeper's wife: ___ Dark
2. Where Beetle found Jane and the baker kissing: Old ___ Road
3. Animals Alyce helped to scrub
4. Magister Reese's book
5. Beetle longed to own it: wood cat ___
6. Will's mother cow
8. Cat's rival in burlap sack in pond
10. Fair held at Goblet-Under-Green: Saint ___'s
12. Beetle watched through these and learned trade
14. Alyce sent him to the manor to do threshing
15. Where Alyce fled
18. Midwife's claim of what Alyce did: ___ up
19. Newly named inn: The Cat and ___
20. How Will describes Alyce
22. Alyce learned to do this from Magister Reese

Midwife's Apprentice Crossword 4

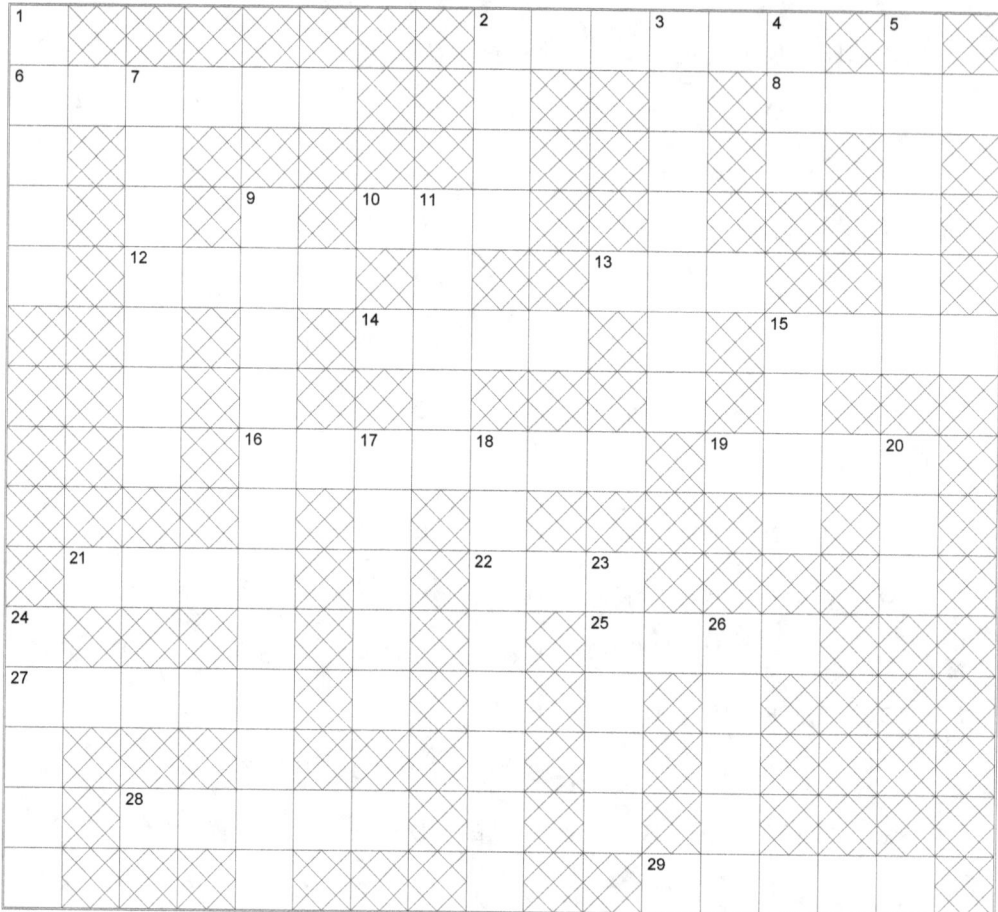

Across
2. Innkeeper's wife: ___ Dark
6. Alyce sent him to the manor to do threshing
8. Town boy Alyce saves
10. Where Alyce fled
12. Warm, rotting muck: ___ heap
13. Best tasting food to Edward
14. Knew no home and no mother
15. Alyce feared taking this
16. Author
19. Midwife's claim of what Alyce did: ___ up
21. Roman goddess of moon, women, and childbirth
22. Will Russet's hair color
25. Mother's whose baby Alyce failed to deliver: ___ Blunt
27. Name for someone who looked like they could read
28. Tansy delivered these
29. Midwife's fault

Down
1. Writer staying at Inn: Magister ___
2. Innkeeper: ___ Dark
3. Brat expected, dreamed, and hoped for this
4. Meals a day for Beetle
5. Beetle bartered for them at the fair
7. Beetle watched through these and learned trade
9. Magister Reese's book
11. Where Beetle found Jane and the baker kissing: Old ___ Road
15. Alyce learned to do this from Magister Reese
17. Animals Alyce helped to scrub
18. Water sold for remedy: ___'s wash
20. Cat's rival in burlap sack in pond
23. Left mysterious footprints
24. Father of thirteen children
26. Where Alyce sent Edward

Midwife's Apprentice Crossword 4 Answer Key

	1 R						2 J	E	3 N	4 N	E	T	5 F	
6 E	D	7 W	A	R	D		O		O	8 W	I	L	L	
	E	I					H		T	O			A	
	S	N		9 E	10 I	11 N	N		H				S	
	E	12 D	U	N	G	O		13 F	I	G			K	
		O			14 C	B	R	A	T	N		15 R	I	S	K
		W			Y		T			G		E		
		16 S		17 C	U	18 S	H	M	A	N		19 G	A	V	20 E
				L		H		U				D		E
	21 J	U	N	O		E		22 R	23 E	D				L
24 B				P		E		D		25 E	M	26 M	A	
27 A	L	Y	C	E		P		E		V		A		
K				D				R		I		N		
E		28 T	W	I	N	S		E		L		O		
R				A				R		29 G	R	E	E	D

Across
2. Innkeeper's wife: ___ Dark
6. Alyce sent him to the manor to do threshing
8. Town boy Alyce saves
10. Where Alyce fled
12. Warm, rotting muck: ___ heap
13. Best tasting food to Edward
14. Knew no home and no mother
15. Alyce feared taking this
16. Author
19. Midwife's claim of what Alyce did: ___ up
21. Roman goddess of moon, women, and childbirth
22. Will Russet's hair color
25. Mother's whose baby Alyce failed to deliver: ___ Blunt
27. Name for someone who looked like they could read
28. Tansy delivered these
29. Midwife's fault

Down
1. Writer staying at Inn: Magister ___
2. Innkeeper: ___ Dark
3. Brat expected, dreamed, and hoped for this
4. Meals a day for Beetle
5. Beetle bartered for them at the fair
7. Beetle watched through these and learned trade
9. Magister Reese's book
11. Where Beetle found Jane and the baker kissing: Old ___ Road
15. Alyce learned to do this from Magister Reese
17. Animals Alyce helped to scrub
18. Water sold for remedy: ___'s wash
20. Cat's rival in burlap sack in pond
23. Left mysterious footprints
24. Father of thirteen children
26. Where Alyce sent Edward

Midwife's Apprentice

MURDERER	DEVIL	PLACE	TWINS	HOOVES
PRETTY	MILLER	SLAPPED	ANKLE	MIDWIFE
CLEAN	DUNG	FREE SPACE	TWO	RED
CUSHMAN	REESE	GROMMET	FLASKS	BRAT
HERBS	BEETLE	FIG	GUTS	INN

Midwife's Apprentice

MANOR	GREASE	SHEEP	ALYCE	EDWARD
FLOOR	EMMA	GREED	APPRENTICE	WINDOWS
SIX	COMB	FREE SPACE	WILL	EEL
CAT	READ	PROSPEROUS	FAILED	PURR
JUNO	SWITHIN	LITTLE	BOYS	SISTER

Midwife's Apprentice

SIX	BAKER	PROSPEROUS	COMB	GREED
CUSHMAN	CAT	PURR	REESE	RISK
MANOR	MIDWIFE	FREE SPACE	PLACE	FLASKS
HERBS	SHEEP	INN	FAILED	SLAPPED
FLOOR	JUNO	DUNG	NORTH	READ

Midwife's Apprentice

EEL	ALYCE	BEETLE	APPRENTICE	MILLER
GREASE	GROMMET	CHEESE	WINDOWS	EMMA
EDWARD	TANSY	FREE SPACE	JENNET	BREAD
TWINS	BRAT	GUTS	HOOVES	ANKLE
LITTLE	MURDERER	RED	CLEAN	NOTHING

Midwife's Apprentice

CHEESE	NOTHING	REESE	TANSY	SHEEP
MIDWIFE	SLAPPED	RED	MILLER	CLEAN
FLOOR	GREED	FREE SPACE	BOYS	ENCYCLOPEDIA
TWO	EEL	GAVE	DUNG	ANKLE
DEVIL	WILL	COMB	HERBS	INN

Midwife's Apprentice

SWITHIN	APPRENTICE	LITTLE	ALYCE	PURR
PLACE	BRAT	PROSPEROUS	EDWARD	JENNET
GREASE	FLASKS	FREE SPACE	HOOVES	WINDOWS
PRETTY	GUTS	TWINS	JOHN	SIX
READ	RISK	BEETLE	NORTH	BREAD

Midwife's Apprentice

LITTLE	FLOOR	PLACE	RISK	PRETTY
CHEESE	SHEEP	EEL	SWITHIN	GREASE
EDWARD	MURDERER	FREE SPACE	SISTER	ALYCE
DUNG	MIDWIFE	TWO	NOTHING	ENCYCLOPEDIA
INN	BEETLE	FLASKS	PROSPEROUS	EMMA

Midwife's Apprentice

CAT	COMB	GREED	BREAD	CLEAN
FAILED	HOOVES	DEVIL	GAVE	WILL
MANOR	WINDOWS	FREE SPACE	HERBS	PURR
TANSY	SIX	GUTS	REESE	JOHN
JUNO	BAKER	FIG	NORTH	JENNET

Midwife's Apprentice

GREASE	EMMA	DEVIL	CUSHMAN	LITTLE
ALYCE	SHEEP	FAILED	BOYS	FLOOR
EDWARD	CAT	FREE SPACE	TWO	PURR
SIX	GUTS	BRAT	PLACE	EEL
INN	CHEESE	DUNG	PRETTY	APPRENTICE

Midwife's Apprentice

PROSPEROUS	NOTHING	CLEAN	RED	NORTH
COMB	FLASKS	HOOVES	GROMMET	MILLER
SLAPPED	MANOR	FREE SPACE	SISTER	BREAD
BEETLE	WINDOWS	JUNO	MURDERER	JENNET
ENCYCLOPEDIA	JOHN	ANKLE	TANSY	WILL

Midwife's Apprentice

DUNG	BREAD	PLACE	INN	BRAT
EDWARD	SIX	JOHN	SHEEP	WINDOWS
READ	ALYCE	FREE SPACE	JUNO	GREASE
CUSHMAN	BOYS	MANOR	GUTS	FAILED
NORTH	SLAPPED	PRETTY	NOTHING	DEVIL

Midwife's Apprentice

WILL	MIDWIFE	FIG	GAVE	MURDERER
EEL	CHEESE	CLEAN	GROMMET	TANSY
CAT	FLOOR	FREE SPACE	PROSPEROUS	RED
HERBS	TWINS	ENCYCLOPEDIA	FLASKS	BAKER
GREED	LITTLE	PURR	EMMA	APPRENTICE

Midwife's Apprentice

PLACE	WILL	DUNG	SISTER	BREAD
EEL	APPRENTICE	GREED	NOTHING	SHEEP
FAILED	COMB	FREE SPACE	GAVE	LITTLE
JENNET	ALYCE	SIX	RISK	FIG
TANSY	MILLER	CUSHMAN	REESE	NORTH

Midwife's Apprentice

SLAPPED	READ	PRETTY	MANOR	JOHN
DEVIL	GROMMET	HOOVES	ENCYCLOPEDIA	BEETLE
TWO	EMMA	FREE SPACE	JUNO	HERBS
GUTS	RED	EDWARD	GREASE	BAKER
WINDOWS	TWINS	BRAT	MURDERER	SWITHIN

Midwife's Apprentice

GREED	DUNG	PURR	READ	TWO
RISK	ENCYCLOPEDIA	JENNET	HOOVES	FAILED
HERBS	FLOOR	FREE SPACE	BRAT	BEETLE
GREASE	TWINS	WILL	FLASKS	ANKLE
NOTHING	TANSY	REESE	EMMA	WINDOWS

Midwife's Apprentice

GAVE	PROSPEROUS	CAT	APPRENTICE	JUNO
NORTH	SIX	MIDWIFE	PLACE	CUSHMAN
FIG	COMB	FREE SPACE	RED	LITTLE
CLEAN	BAKER	BREAD	MILLER	ALYCE
MANOR	PRETTY	BOYS	SWITHIN	SHEEP

Midwife's Apprentice

DUNG	INN	WILL	HOOVES	BRAT
JUNO	BOYS	MURDERER	CUSHMAN	ENCYCLOPEDIA
APPRENTICE	ANKLE	FREE SPACE	SISTER	GAVE
MIDWIFE	TWO	JOHN	JENNET	NOTHING
RED	SLAPPED	CHEESE	ALYCE	REESE

Midwife's Apprentice

BAKER	CAT	GUTS	PURR	GREASE
MILLER	BREAD	HERBS	NORTH	RISK
DEVIL	GREED	FREE SPACE	READ	FLASKS
EEL	TWINS	SIX	LITTLE	MANOR
WINDOWS	SWITHIN	GROMMET	FLOOR	EMMA

Midwife's Apprentice

MURDERER	TANSY	TWINS	JOHN	FLASKS
RED	COMB	MIDWIFE	FIG	RISK
BRAT	WINDOWS	FREE SPACE	HERBS	NOTHING
SIX	DUNG	NORTH	GREED	CAT
GUTS	BOYS	JUNO	APPRENTICE	JENNET

Midwife's Apprentice

REESE	GAVE	PURR	SLAPPED	EDWARD
EMMA	SISTER	ALYCE	CUSHMAN	PRETTY
PROSPEROUS	BREAD	FREE SPACE	CHEESE	ENCYCLOPEDIA
LITTLE	EEL	GROMMET	MANOR	SWITHIN
INN	GREASE	SHEEP	BEETLE	TWO

Midwife's Apprentice

GUTS	SHEEP	FLASKS	FLOOR	PRETTY
EMMA	HERBS	PLACE	EEL	DEVIL
REESE	GROMMET	FREE SPACE	GAVE	GREED
CHEESE	SWITHIN	INN	COMB	EDWARD
MIDWIFE	GREASE	WINDOWS	RISK	JENNET

Midwife's Apprentice

NORTH	READ	FIG	MANOR	APPRENTICE
MILLER	JOHN	CUSHMAN	PROSPEROUS	SIX
MURDERER	TWINS	FREE SPACE	CLEAN	LITTLE
BOYS	BREAD	ALYCE	HOOVES	DUNG
BEETLE	FAILED	RED	NOTHING	BAKER

Midwife's Apprentice

CLEAN	WINDOWS	MIDWIFE	SHEEP	MURDERER
ANKLE	HERBS	EEL	JENNET	SIX
RED	REESE	FREE SPACE	BREAD	COMB
NORTH	INN	HOOVES	BRAT	GROMMET
WILL	PURR	FLASKS	PROSPEROUS	READ

Midwife's Apprentice

ENCYCLOPEDIA	EMMA	FLOOR	DUNG	BOYS
TWINS	PRETTY	TANSY	JOHN	GREASE
SLAPPED	BAKER	FREE SPACE	GUTS	EDWARD
GREED	GAVE	JUNO	SISTER	NOTHING
MANOR	LITTLE	FAILED	ALYCE	MILLER

Midwife's Apprentice

BREAD	EEL	FLOOR	COMB	EMMA
GREED	HERBS	LITTLE	CLEAN	NORTH
READ	TWO	FREE SPACE	HOOVES	ENCYCLOPEDIA
PRETTY	SHEEP	RISK	ALYCE	SIX
BAKER	REESE	INN	TWINS	FIG

Midwife's Apprentice

SISTER	CHEESE	GUTS	JUNO	JOHN
RED	PROSPEROUS	CAT	GAVE	MIDWIFE
JENNET	GROMMET	FREE SPACE	CUSHMAN	PLACE
BRAT	MANOR	DEVIL	WINDOWS	DUNG
ANKLE	BEETLE	NOTHING	GREASE	APPRENTICE

Midwife's Apprentice

FLOOR	CUSHMAN	SISTER	SHEEP	NOTHING
CAT	REESE	WINDOWS	PLACE	DUNG
TANSY	SLAPPED	FREE SPACE	SIX	GREASE
FLASKS	CHEESE	MIDWIFE	ALYCE	HERBS
BOYS	EEL	LITTLE	COMB	INN

Midwife's Apprentice

MURDERER	GAVE	PRETTY	CLEAN	NORTH
TWINS	RED	MILLER	TWO	EDWARD
MANOR	RISK	FREE SPACE	PURR	HOOVES
ENCYCLOPEDIA	FIG	WILL	BEETLE	JENNET
ANKLE	GROMMET	APPRENTICE	DEVIL	BREAD

Midwife's Apprentice

BRAT	GROMMET	JOHN	GREASE	FLASKS
JENNET	FAILED	PRETTY	MILLER	SIX
WILL	GREED	FREE SPACE	DUNG	FLOOR
PLACE	CHEESE	MIDWIFE	GUTS	TANSY
SHEEP	GAVE	CLEAN	BOYS	EEL

Midwife's Apprentice

BREAD	HERBS	RISK	TWO	DEVIL
WINDOWS	EDWARD	BEETLE	COMB	ANKLE
RED	APPRENTICE	FREE SPACE	LITTLE	ENCYCLOPEDIA
REESE	MANOR	ALYCE	CUSHMAN	TWINS
SISTER	EMMA	FIG	JUNO	HOOVES

Midwife's Apprentice

EEL	GROMMET	ALYCE	JOHN	WILL
FIG	REESE	MANOR	FLOOR	APPRENTICE
NOTHING	TWINS	FREE SPACE	HOOVES	RED
NORTH	PROSPEROUS	FAILED	LITTLE	BREAD
READ	EDWARD	MURDERER	PRETTY	GAVE

Midwife's Apprentice

HERBS	ANKLE	MIDWIFE	CUSHMAN	EMMA
JENNET	MILLER	RISK	BEETLE	FLASKS
BRAT	PURR	FREE SPACE	PLACE	DUNG
GREED	CAT	CLEAN	TWO	SIX
DEVIL	SWITHIN	SISTER	ENCYCLOPEDIA	SHEEP

Midwife's Apprentice Vocabulary Word List

No.	Word	Clue/Definition
1.	ABBEY	Convent; monastery
2.	ABUNDANCE	Plenty
3.	ANTIPODES	Uninhabited islands S. E. of New Zealand
4.	BAILIFF	Arresting officer
5.	BERATING	Scolding
6.	BLIGHT	Curse
7.	CHRISTENED	Named
8.	COMPASSION	Sympathy; caring
9.	COMPENDIUM	Comprehensive summary
10.	DECEIT	Dishonesty
11.	DESOLATE	Deserted; abandoned
12.	DIRE	Dreadful; awful
13.	DISREPUTE	Dishonor
14.	EFFICACY	Effectiveness; capability
15.	EXERTIONS	Efforts; labors
16.	FERMENTING	Ripening
17.	GLUTTONY	Excessive overeating
18.	HAGGLING	Bartering; dickering
19.	HEEDLESS	Unmindful
20.	HENCEFORTH	From now on
21.	HOIST	Lift up
22.	IGNORANCE	Unawareness; inexperience
23.	INCOMPETENCE	Stupidity; inability
24.	INNOVATION	An improvement
25.	LUXURIOUS	Rich; fine
26.	MEANDERED	Rambled
27.	MEWLING	Whimpering; whining
28.	NIMBLE	Lively; quick
29.	PATERNOSTERS	Parts of the Lord's Prayer
30.	PLUCK	Spirit; spunk
31.	PRIVY	An outhouse
32.	PROSPEROUS	Well-to-do
33.	REASSURE	Encourage; inspire
34.	RELUCTANT	Unwilling
35.	RENOWNED	Famous
36.	REPLENISH	Restock
37.	RESISTANCE	Opposition
38.	RESOUNDED	Echoed
39.	REVELERS	Drinkers; carousers
40.	SOLEMNITY	Seriousness
41.	SOOTHSAYERS	Prophets; fortunetellers
42.	STANCHING	Stopping the flow
43.	STOUT	Heavy set
44.	STUPEFIED	Astonished; shocked
45.	SULLEN	Silent
46.	SUNDRY	Many; numerous
47.	TANTALIZING	Fascinating
48.	TAUNTED	Mocked; sneered
49.	THRASHED	Tossed violently about
50.	THRESHING	Beating grain to separate seeds from stalk
51.	TREACHERY	Betrayal; disloyalty

Copyrighted

Midwife's Apprentice Vocabulary Word List

No.	Word	Clue/Definition
52.	TRIUMPHANT	Victorious
53.	TUMULT	Turmoil
54.	TWEAKED	A sharp pull or twist
55.	VICTORIOUS	Successful
56.	VIGOROUS	Energetic
57.	WIMPLE	Woman's headcloth drawn in folds about the chin
58.	WRITHING	Turning and twisting from pain

Midwife's Apprentice Vocabulary Fill In The Blanks 1

_____ 1. Stupidity; inability

_____ 2. Echoed

_____ 3. Turning and twisting from pain

_____ 4. From now on

_____ 5. Lift up

_____ 6. Uninhabited islands S. E. of New Zealand

_____ 7. Unmindful

_____ 8. Convent; monastery

_____ 9. Victorious

_____ 10. Arresting officer

_____ 11. Effectiveness; capability

_____ 12. Silent

_____ 13. Lively; quick

_____ 14. Unawareness; inexperience

_____ 15. Excessive overeating

_____ 16. A sharp pull or twist

_____ 17. Parts of the Lord's Prayer

_____ 18. Energetic

_____ 19. Astonished; shocked

_____ 20. Prophets; fortunetellers

Midwife's Apprentice Vocabulary Fill In The Blanks 1 Answer Key

INCOMPETENCE	1. Stupidity; inability
RESOUNDED	2. Echoed
WRITHING	3. Turning and twisting from pain
HENCEFORTH	4. From now on
HOIST	5. Lift up
ANTIPODES	6. Uninhabited islands S. E. of New Zealand
HEEDLESS	7. Unmindful
ABBEY	8. Convent; monastery
TRIUMPHANT	9. Victorious
BAILIFF	10. Arresting officer
EFFICACY	11. Effectiveness; capability
SULLEN	12. Silent
NIMBLE	13. Lively; quick
IGNORANCE	14. Unawareness; inexperience
GLUTTONY	15. Excessive overeating
TWEAKED	16. A sharp pull or twist
PATERNOSTERS	17. Parts of the Lord's Prayer
VIGOROUS	18. Energetic
STUPEFIED	19. Astonished; shocked
SOOTHSAYERS	20. Prophets; fortunetellers

Midwife's Apprentice Vocabulary Fill In The Blanks 2

_____ 1. Woman's headcloth drawn in folds about the chin

_____ 2. Bartering; dickering

_____ 3. Unawareness; inexperience

_____ 4. Effectiveness; capability

_____ 5. Parts of the Lord's Prayer

_____ 6. Opposition

_____ 7. Energetic

_____ 8. Deserted; abandoned

_____ 9. Stupidity; inability

_____ 10. Echoed

_____ 11. Curse

_____ 12. Rich; fine

_____ 13. Uninhabited islands S. E. of New Zealand

_____ 14. A sharp pull or twist

_____ 15. Lift up

_____ 16. Dreadful; awful

_____ 17. Unwilling

_____ 18. Rambled

_____ 19. An improvement

_____ 20. Fascinating

Midwife's Apprentice Vocabulary Fill In The Blanks 2 Answer Key

WIMPLE	1. Woman's headcloth drawn in folds about the chin
HAGGLING	2. Bartering; dickering
IGNORANCE	3. Unawareness; inexperience
EFFICACY	4. Effectiveness; capability
PATERNOSTERS	5. Parts of the Lord's Prayer
RESISTANCE	6. Opposition
VIGOROUS	7. Energetic
DESOLATE	8. Deserted; abandoned
INCOMPETENCE	9. Stupidity; inability
RESOUNDED	10. Echoed
BLIGHT	11. Curse
LUXURIOUS	12. Rich; fine
ANTIPODES	13. Uninhabited islands S. E. of New Zealand
TWEAKED	14. A sharp pull or twist
HOIST	15. Lift up
DIRE	16. Dreadful; awful
RELUCTANT	17. Unwilling
MEANDERED	18. Rambled
INNOVATION	19. An improvement
TANTALIZING	20. Fascinating

Midwife's Apprentice Vocabulary Fill In The Blanks 3

_____   1. Dishonesty

_____   2. Scolding

_____   3. Betrayal; disloyalty

_____   4. Mocked; sneered

_____   5. Beating grain to separate seeds from stalk

_____   6. An outhouse

_____   7. Plenty

_____   8. Unawareness; inexperience

_____   9. Comprehensive summary

_____   10. Arresting officer

_____   11. Ripening

_____   12. Sympathy; caring

_____   13. Prophets; fortunetellers

_____   14. Turmoil

_____   15. Unwilling

_____   16. Tossed violently about

_____   17. Woman's headcloth drawn in folds about the chin

_____   18. Convent; monastery

_____   19. Victorious

_____   20. From now on

Midwife's Apprentice Vocabulary Fill In The Blanks 3 Answer Key

DECEIT	1. Dishonesty
BERATING	2. Scolding
TREACHERY	3. Betrayal; disloyalty
TAUNTED	4. Mocked; sneered
THRESHING	5. Beating grain to separate seeds from stalk
PRIVY	6. An outhouse
ABUNDANCE	7. Plenty
IGNORANCE	8. Unawareness; inexperience
COMPENDIUM	9. Comprehensive summary
BAILIFF	10. Arresting officer
FERMENTING	11. Ripening
COMPASSION	12. Sympathy; caring
SOOTHSAYERS	13. Prophets; fortunetellers
TUMULT	14. Turmoil
RELUCTANT	15. Unwilling
THRASHED	16. Tossed violently about
WIMPLE	17. Woman's headcloth drawn in folds about the chin
ABBEY	18. Convent; monastery
TRIUMPHANT	19. Victorious
HENCEFORTH	20. From now on

Midwife's Apprentice Vocabulary Fill In The Blanks 4

_____   1. Parts of the Lord's Prayer

_____   2. Drinkers; carousers

_____   3. Unmindful

_____   4. An outhouse

_____   5. Beating grain to separate seeds from stalk

_____   6. Echoed

_____   7. A sharp pull or twist

_____   8. Dishonesty

_____   9. Comprehensive summary

_____   10. Turmoil

_____   11. Silent

_____   12. Excessive overeating

_____   13. Astonished; shocked

_____   14. Convent; monastery

_____   15. Prophets; fortunetellers

_____   16. Stupidity; inability

_____   17. Plenty

_____   18. Rich; fine

_____   19. Deserted; abandoned

_____   20. Seriousness

Midwife's Apprentice Vocabulary Fill In The Blanks 4 Answer Key

PATERNOSTERS	1. Parts of the Lord's Prayer
REVELERS	2. Drinkers; carousers
HEEDLESS	3. Unmindful
PRIVY	4. An outhouse
THRESHING	5. Beating grain to separate seeds from stalk
RESOUNDED	6. Echoed
TWEAKED	7. A sharp pull or twist
DECEIT	8. Dishonesty
COMPENDIUM	9. Comprehensive summary
TUMULT	10. Turmoil
SULLEN	11. Silent
GLUTTONY	12. Excessive overeating
STUPEFIED	13. Astonished; shocked
ABBEY	14. Convent; monastery
SOOTHSAYERS	15. Prophets; fortunetellers
INCOMPETENCE	16. Stupidity; inability
ABUNDANCE	17. Plenty
LUXURIOUS	18. Rich; fine
DESOLATE	19. Deserted; abandoned
SOLEMNITY	20. Seriousness

Copyrighted

Midwife's Apprentice Vocabulary Matching 1

___ 1. PRIVY   A. Well-to-do
___ 2. NIMBLE   B. Named
___ 3. VICTORIOUS   C. Spirit; spunk
___ 4. REVELERS   D. Unawareness; inexperience
___ 5. TUMULT   E. Prophets; fortunetellers
___ 6. TREACHERY   F. Rambled
___ 7. PLUCK   G. Victorious
___ 8. PROSPEROUS   H. Curse
___ 9. STOUT   I. Drinkers; carousers
___10. RENOWNED   J. Turmoil
___11. INCOMPETENCE   K. Opposition
___12. SOOTHSAYERS   L. Famous
___13. COMPASSION   M. Woman's headcloth drawn in folds about the chin
___14. WIMPLE   N. Betrayal; disloyalty
___15. IGNORANCE   O. Sympathy; caring
___16. DISREPUTE   P. Stupidity; inability
___17. CHRISTENED   Q. Heavy set
___18. TRIUMPHANT   R. Uninhabited islands S. E. of New Zealand
___19. THRESHING   S. Successful
___20. HENCEFORTH   T. From now on
___21. ANTIPODES   U. Lively; quick
___22. LUXURIOUS   V. Dishonor
___23. MEANDERED   W. Rich; fine
___24. RESISTANCE   X. Beating grain to separate seeds from stalk
___25. BLIGHT   Y. An outhouse

Midwife's Apprentice Vocabulary Matching 1 Answer Key

Y - 1. PRIVY
U - 2. NIMBLE
S - 3. VICTORIOUS
I - 4. REVELERS
J - 5. TUMULT
N - 6. TREACHERY
C - 7. PLUCK
A - 8. PROSPEROUS
Q - 9. STOUT
L - 10. RENOWNED
P - 11. INCOMPETENCE
E - 12. SOOTHSAYERS
O - 13. COMPASSION
M - 14. WIMPLE
D - 15. IGNORANCE
V - 16. DISREPUTE
B - 17. CHRISTENED
G - 18. TRIUMPHANT
X - 19. THRESHING
T - 20. HENCEFORTH
R - 21. ANTIPODES
W - 22. LUXURIOUS
F - 23. MEANDERED
K - 24. RESISTANCE
H - 25. BLIGHT

A. Well-to-do
B. Named
C. Spirit; spunk
D. Unawareness; inexperience
E. Prophets; fortunetellers
F. Rambled
G. Victorious
H. Curse
I. Drinkers; carousers
J. Turmoil
K. Opposition
L. Famous
M. Woman's headcloth drawn in folds about the chin
N. Betrayal; disloyalty
O. Sympathy; caring
P. Stupidity; inability
Q. Heavy set
R. Uninhabited islands S. E. of New Zealand
S. Successful
T. From now on
U. Lively; quick
V. Dishonor
W. Rich; fine
X. Beating grain to separate seeds from stalk
Y. An outhouse

Midwife's Apprentice Vocabulary Matching 2

___ 1. MEANDERED   A. Many; numerous
___ 2. HENCEFORTH   B. Bartering; dickering
___ 3. THRESHING   C. Comprehensive summary
___ 4. COMPENDIUM   D. Mocked; sneered
___ 5. TANTALIZING   E. Tossed violently about
___ 6. WIMPLE   F. Parts of the Lord's Prayer
___ 7. THRASHED   G. Uninhabited islands S. E. of New Zealand
___ 8. VIGOROUS   H. Turning and twisting from pain
___ 9. SUNDRY   I. Energetic
___ 10. DECEIT   J. Unwilling
___ 11. HAGGLING   K. Encourage; inspire
___ 12. TAUNTED   L. Fascinating
___ 13. STUPEFIED   M. Astonished; shocked
___ 14. DESOLATE   N. Deserted; abandoned
___ 15. RELUCTANT   O. From now on
___ 16. REASSURE   P. Well-to-do
___ 17. CHRISTENED   Q. Rambled
___ 18. PATERNOSTERS R. Beating grain to separate seeds from stalk
___ 19. PROSPEROUS   S. Named
___ 20. ANTIPODES   T. Silent
___ 21. SULLEN   U. Dishonesty
___ 22. TWEAKED   V. Lively; quick
___ 23. BAILIFF   W. Woman's headcloth drawn in folds about the chin
___ 24. NIMBLE   X. A sharp pull or twist
___ 25. WRITHING   Y. Arresting officer

Midwife's Apprentice Vocabulary Matching 2 Answer Key

Q - 1. MEANDERED	A.	Many; numerous
O - 2. HENCEFORTH	B.	Bartering; dickering
R - 3. THRESHING	C.	Comprehensive summary
C - 4. COMPENDIUM	D.	Mocked; sneered
L - 5. TANTALIZING	E.	Tossed violently about
W - 6. WIMPLE	F.	Parts of the Lord's Prayer
E - 7. THRASHED	G.	Uninhabited islands S. E. of New Zealand
I - 8. VIGOROUS	H.	Turning and twisting from pain
A - 9. SUNDRY	I.	Energetic
U - 10. DECEIT	J.	Unwilling
B - 11. HAGGLING	K.	Encourage; inspire
D - 12. TAUNTED	L.	Fascinating
M - 13. STUPEFIED	M.	Astonished; shocked
N - 14. DESOLATE	N.	Deserted; abandoned
J - 15. RELUCTANT	O.	From now on
K - 16. REASSURE	P.	Well-to-do
S - 17. CHRISTENED	Q.	Rambled
F - 18. PATERNOSTERS	R.	Beating grain to separate seeds from stalk
P - 19. PROSPEROUS	S.	Named
G - 20. ANTIPODES	T.	Silent
T - 21. SULLEN	U.	Dishonesty
X - 22. TWEAKED	V.	Lively; quick
Y - 23. BAILIFF	W.	Woman's headcloth drawn in folds about the chin
V - 24. NIMBLE	X.	A sharp pull or twist
H - 25. WRITHING	Y.	Arresting officer

Midwife's Apprentice Vocabulary Matching 3

___ 1. GLUTTONY   A. Successful
___ 2. PLUCK   B. Seriousness
___ 3. RENOWNED   C. Dishonor
___ 4. HEEDLESS   D. Astonished; shocked
___ 5. VICTORIOUS   E. Ripening
___ 6. ANTIPODES   F. Fascinating
___ 7. STANCHING   G. From now on
___ 8. DISREPUTE   H. Stopping the flow
___ 9. HENCEFORTH   I. Unmindful
___10. BERATING   J. Spirit; spunk
___11. CHRISTENED   K. Scolding
___12. TREACHERY   L. Rambled
___13. MEANDERED   M. Heavy set
___14. FERMENTING   N. Silent
___15. STUPEFIED   O. Betrayal; disloyalty
___16. STOUT   P. Famous
___17. DECEIT   Q. Efforts; labors
___18. SULLEN   R. Comprehensive summary
___19. HAGGLING   S. Bartering; dickering
___20. INNOVATION   T. Many; numerous
___21. TANTALIZING   U. Named
___22. SUNDRY   V. Dishonesty
___23. SOLEMNITY   W. Excessive overeating
___24. EXERTIONS   X. Uninhabited islands S. E. of New Zealand
___25. COMPENDIUM   Y. An improvement

Midwife's Apprentice Vocabulary Matching 3 Answer Key

W - 1. GLUTTONY
J - 2. PLUCK
P - 3. RENOWNED
I - 4. HEEDLESS
A - 5. VICTORIOUS
X - 6. ANTIPODES
H - 7. STANCHING
C - 8. DISREPUTE
G - 9. HENCEFORTH
K - 10. BERATING
U - 11. CHRISTENED
O - 12. TREACHERY
L - 13. MEANDERED
E - 14. FERMENTING
D - 15. STUPEFIED
M - 16. STOUT
V - 17. DECEIT
N - 18. SULLEN
S - 19. HAGGLING
Y - 20. INNOVATION
F - 21. TANTALIZING
T - 22. SUNDRY
B - 23. SOLEMNITY
Q - 24. EXERTIONS
R - 25. COMPENDIUM

A. Successful
B. Seriousness
C. Dishonor
D. Astonished; shocked
E. Ripening
F. Fascinating
G. From now on
H. Stopping the flow
I. Unmindful
J. Spirit; spunk
K. Scolding
L. Rambled
M. Heavy set
N. Silent
O. Betrayal; disloyalty
P. Famous
Q. Efforts; labors
R. Comprehensive summary
S. Bartering; dickering
T. Many; numerous
U. Named
V. Dishonesty
W. Excessive overeating
X. Uninhabited islands S. E. of New Zealand
Y. An improvement

Midwife's Apprentice Vocabulary Matching 4

___ 1. TAUNTED A. Restock
___ 2. DISREPUTE B. An improvement
___ 3. BLIGHT C. Many; numerous
___ 4. STANCHING D. Woman's headcloth drawn in folds about the chin
___ 5. THRASHED E. Uninhabited islands S. E. of New Zealand
___ 6. WIMPLE F. Tossed violently about
___ 7. ANTIPODES G. Plenty
___ 8. HENCEFORTH H. Deserted; abandoned
___ 9. GLUTTONY I. From now on
___ 10. NIMBLE J. Bartering; dickering
___ 11. INNOVATION K. Excessive overeating
___ 12. INCOMPETENCE L. Efforts; labors
___ 13. EXERTIONS M. Curse
___ 14. STOUT N. Stupidity; inability
___ 15. HAGGLING O. Dishonor
___ 16. HOIST P. Stopping the flow
___ 17. ABUNDANCE Q. Mocked; sneered
___ 18. ABBEY R. Unmindful
___ 19. SUNDRY S. Convent; monastery
___ 20. IGNORANCE T. Heavy set
___ 21. PROSPEROUS U. Lively; quick
___ 22. REPLENISH V. Famous
___ 23. RENOWNED W. Lift up
___ 24. HEEDLESS X. Well-to-do
___ 25. DESOLATE Y. Unawareness; inexperience

Midwife's Apprentice Vocabulary Matching 4 Answer Key

Q - 1. TAUNTED	A.	Restock
O - 2. DISREPUTE	B.	An improvement
M - 3. BLIGHT	C.	Many; numerous
P - 4. STANCHING	D.	Woman's headcloth drawn in folds about the chin
F - 5. THRASHED	E.	Uninhabited islands S. E. of New Zealand
D - 6. WIMPLE	F.	Tossed violently about
E - 7. ANTIPODES	G.	Plenty
I - 8. HENCEFORTH	H.	Deserted; abandoned
K - 9. GLUTTONY	I.	From now on
U - 10. NIMBLE	J.	Bartering; dickering
B - 11. INNOVATION	K.	Excessive overeating
N - 12. INCOMPETENCE	L.	Efforts; labors
L - 13. EXERTIONS	M.	Curse
T - 14. STOUT	N.	Stupidity; inability
J - 15. HAGGLING	O.	Dishonor
W - 16. HOIST	P.	Stopping the flow
G - 17. ABUNDANCE	Q.	Mocked; sneered
S - 18. ABBEY	R.	Unmindful
C - 19. SUNDRY	S.	Convent; monastery
Y - 20. IGNORANCE	T.	Heavy set
X - 21. PROSPEROUS	U.	Lively; quick
A - 22. REPLENISH	V.	Famous
V - 23. RENOWNED	W.	Lift up
R - 24. HEEDLESS	X.	Well-to-do
H - 25. DESOLATE	Y.	Unawareness; inexperience

Midwife's Apprentice Vocabulary Magic Squares 1

Match the definition with the vocabulary word. Put your answers in the magic squares below. When your answers are correct, all columns and rows will add to the same number.

A. HAGGLING
B. WIMPLE
C. INCOMPETENCE
D. DECEIT
E. PROSPEROUS
F. SUNDRY
G. RESOUNDED
H. PATERNOSTERS
I. PRIVY
J. SOLEMNITY
K. HEEDLESS
L. HENCEFORTH
M. RENOWNED
N. PLUCK
O. STUPEFIED
P. COMPENDIUM

1. Parts of the Lord's Prayer
2. Famous
3. Woman's headcloth drawn in folds about the chin
4. Unmindful
5. Seriousness
6. Stupidity; inability
7. Comprehensive summary
8. Well-to-do
9. Astonished; shocked
10. Many; numerous
11. An outhouse
12. Dishonesty
13. Bartering; dickering
14. From now on
15. Echoed
16. Spirit; spunk

A=	B=	C=	D=
E=	F=	G=	H=
I=	J=	K=	L=
M=	N=	O=	P=

Midwife's Apprentice Vocabulary Magic Squares 1 Answer Key

Match the definition with the vocabulary word. Put your answers in the magic squares below. When your answers are correct, all columns and rows will add to the same number.

A. HAGGLING
B. WIMPLE
C. INCOMPETENCE
D. DECEIT
E. PROSPEROUS
F. SUNDRY
G. RESOUNDED
H. PATERNOSTERS
I. PRIVY
J. SOLEMNITY
K. HEEDLESS
L. HENCEFORTH
M. RENOWNED
N. PLUCK
O. STUPEFIED
P. COMPENDIUM

1. Parts of the Lord's Prayer
2. Famous
3. Woman's headcloth drawn in folds about the chin
4. Unmindful
5. Seriousness
6. Stupidity; inability
7. Comprehensive summary
8. Well-to-do
9. Astonished; shocked
10. Many; numerous
11. An outhouse
12. Dishonesty
13. Bartering; dickering
14. From now on
15. Echoed
16. Spirit; spunk

A=13	B=3	C=6	D=12
E=8	F=10	G=15	H=1
I=11	J=5	K=4	L=14
M=2	N=16	O=9	P=7

Midwife's Apprentice Vocabulary Magic Squares 2

Match the definition with the vocabulary word. Put your answers in the magic squares below. When your answers are correct, all columns and rows will add to the same number.

A. IGNORANCE
B. INCOMPETENCE
C. RENOWNED
D. RESISTANCE
E. DISREPUTE
F. REASSURE
G. TRIUMPHANT
H. STOUT
I. INNOVATION
J. TAUNTED
K. WRITHING
L. BLIGHT
M. THRASHED
N. THRESHING
O. VICTORIOUS
P. GLUTTONY

1. Heavy set
2. Unawareness; inexperience
3. Stupidity; inability
4. Victorious
5. Mocked; sneered
6. Successful
7. Excessive overeating
8. An improvement
9. Turning and twisting from pain
10. Beating grain to separate seeds from stalk
11. Tossed violently about
12. Curse
13. Dishonor
14. Opposition
15. Famous
16. Encourage; inspire

A=	B=	C=	D=
E=	F=	G=	H=
I=	J=	K=	L=
M=	N=	O=	P=

Midwife's Apprentice Vocabulary Magic Squares 2 Answer Key

Match the definition with the vocabulary word. Put your answers in the magic squares below. When your answers are correct, all columns and rows will add to the same number.

A. IGNORANCE
B. INCOMPETENCE
C. RENOWNED
D. RESISTANCE
E. DISREPUTE
F. REASSURE
G. TRIUMPHANT
H. STOUT
I. INNOVATION
J. TAUNTED
K. WRITHING
L. BLIGHT
M. THRASHED
N. THRESHING
O. VICTORIOUS
P. GLUTTONY

1. Heavy set
2. Unawareness; inexperience
3. Stupidity; inability
4. Victorious
5. Mocked; sneered
6. Successful
7. Excessive overeating
8. An improvement
9. Turning and twisting from pain
10. Beating grain to separate seeds from stalk
11. Tossed violently about
12. Curse
13. Dishonor
14. Opposition
15. Famous
16. Encourage; inspire

A=2	B=3	C=15	D=14
E=13	F=16	G=4	H=1
I=8	J=5	K=9	L=12
M=11	N=10	O=6	P=7

Midwife's Apprentice Vocabulary Magic Squares 3

Match the definition with the vocabulary word. Put your answers in the magic squares below. When your answers are correct, all columns and rows will add to the same number.

A. SULLEN
B. STUPEFIED
C. TANTALIZING
D. RENOWNED
E. SUNDRY
F. REPLENISH
G. REVELERS
H. TRIUMPHANT
I. FERMENTING
J. SOLEMNITY
K. INNOVATION
L. THRESHING
M. HEEDLESS
N. THRASHED
O. BERATING
P. PLUCK

1. Scolding
2. Famous
3. Seriousness
4. Many; numerous
5. Ripening
6. Restock
7. Spirit; spunk
8. Fascinating
9. Victorious
10. An improvement
11. Silent
12. Tossed violently about
13. Astonished; shocked
14. Unmindful
15. Drinkers; carousers
16. Beating grain to separate seeds from stalk

A=	B=	C=	D=
E=	F=	G=	H=
I=	J=	K=	L=
M=	N=	O=	P=

Midwife's Apprentice Vocabulary Magic Squares 3 Answer Key

Match the definition with the vocabulary word. Put your answers in the magic squares below. When your answers are correct, all columns and rows will add to the same number.

A. SULLEN
B. STUPEFIED
C. TANTALIZING
D. RENOWNED
E. SUNDRY
F. REPLENISH
G. REVELERS
H. TRIUMPHANT
I. FERMENTING
J. SOLEMNITY
K. INNOVATION
L. THRESHING
M. HEEDLESS
N. THRASHED
O. BERATING
P. PLUCK

1. Scolding
2. Famous
3. Seriousness
4. Many; numerous
5. Ripening
6. Restock
7. Spirit; spunk
8. Fascinating
9. Victorious
10. An improvement
11. Silent
12. Tossed violently about
13. Astonished; shocked
14. Unmindful
15. Drinkers; carousers
16. Beating grain to separate seeds from stalk

A=11	B=13	C=8	D=2
E=4	F=6	G=15	H=9
I=5	J=3	K=10	L=16
M=14	N=12	O=1	P=7

Midwife's Apprentice Vocabulary Magic Squares 4

Match the definition with the vocabulary word. Put your answers in the magic squares below. When your answers are correct, all columns and rows will add to the same number.

A. SUNDRY
B. REASSURE
C. TUMULT
D. TWEAKED
E. PROSPEROUS
F. IGNORANCE
G. NIMBLE
H. RENOWNED
I. HAGGLING
J. REVELERS
K. VICTORIOUS
L. PLUCK
M. FERMENTING
N. VIGOROUS
O. BLIGHT
P. HOIST

1. Encourage; inspire
2. Lively; quick
3. Successful
4. Energetic
5. Ripening
6. Spirit; spunk
7. Famous
8. Many; numerous
9. Lift up
10. Bartering; dickering
11. Well-to-do
12. A sharp pull or twist
13. Turmoil
14. Unawareness; inexperience
15. Drinkers; carousers
16. Curse

A=	B=	C=	D=
E=	F=	G=	H=
I=	J=	K=	L=
M=	N=	O=	P=

Midwife's Apprentice Vocabulary Magic Squares 4 Answer Key

Match the definition with the vocabulary word. Put your answers in the magic squares below. When your answers are correct, all columns and rows will add to the same number.

A. SUNDRY
B. REASSURE
C. TUMULT
D. TWEAKED
E. PROSPEROUS
F. IGNORANCE
G. NIMBLE
H. RENOWNED
I. HAGGLING
J. REVELERS
K. VICTORIOUS
L. PLUCK
M. FERMENTING
N. VIGOROUS
O. BLIGHT
P. HOIST

1. Encourage; inspire
2. Lively; quick
3. Successful
4. Energetic
5. Ripening
6. Spirit; spunk
7. Famous
8. Many; numerous
9. Lift up
10. Bartering; dickering
11. Well-to-do
12. A sharp pull or twist
13. Turmoil
14. Unawareness; inexperience
15. Drinkers; carousers
16. Curse

A=8	B=1	C=13	D=12
E=11	F=14	G=2	H=7
I=10	J=15	K=3	L=6
M=5	N=4	O=16	P=9

Midwife's Apprentice Vocabulary Word Search 1

Words are placed backwards, forward, diagonally, up and down. Clues listed below can help you find the words. Circle the hidden vocabulary words in the maze.

```
E X E R T I O N S W B A I L I F F T H B
B L I G H T H I Y R E G F C M M W Z S R
R C B M Z G C M M I R A Q P Q E L V P L
E E D Z H B W B T T A B M J A W W N C W
C D V L A Y Y L R H T U D K M L V O H P
N Y S E Y N V E I I I N E Z E I G I R M
A C W L L H T P U N N D I J A N M T I F
T A D H S E X I M G G A F W N G V A S D
S C E S O T R S P L X N C P M E I G O E R
I I T H O G F S H O Z C D E U P R E N Q
S F N O T S L G A C D E E T L E C O N E B
E F U I H G H U N P Z E L O S E D E R I D S
R E A S S U R E T A L O S R Y T D A E E Y
Y V T T A Z E W P T L D O Z N U J D N S Y
K H O T Y W P T L L H R L N P K E W C U N P
S U R U E Y Y E D O J X E Y H O H E N U K
T U S M R Y Y L N G B S R N S N Y S R D O S
M A L U S L P R I V Y S B A E S F V Q R S H
X B Y L P R I V Y S P I H R R F L S C D Y E F
S B N T E V S P I H R R F L S C D Y E F
S E Z J X N H D P H K T R E A C H E R Y
P Y N D P P L T T R E L U C T A N T N Q
```

A sharp pull or twist (7)
An improvement (10)
An outhouse (5)
Arresting officer (7)
Astonished; shocked (9)
Betrayal; disloyalty (9)
Convent; monastery (5)
Curse (6)
Deserted; abandoned (8)
Dishonesty (6)
Dishonor (9)
Dreadful; awful (4)
Drinkers; carousers (8)
Echoed (9)
Effectiveness; capability (8)
Efforts; labors (9)
Encourage; inspire (8)
Energetic (8)
Excessive overeating (8)
Famous (8)
Heavy set (5)
Lift up (5)
Lively; quick (6)

Many; numerous (6)
Mocked; sneered (7)
Named (10)
Opposition (10)
Plenty (9)
Prophets; fortunetellers (11)
Rambled (9)
Restock (9)
Scolding (8)
Silent (6)
Spirit; spunk (5)
Tossed violently about (8)
Turmoil (6)
Turning and twisting from pain (8)
Unawareness; inexperience (9)
Uninhabited islands S. E. of New Zealand (9)
Unmindful (8)
Unwilling (9)
Victorious (10)
Whimpering; whining (7)
Woman's headcloth drawn in folds about the chin (6)

Midwife's Apprentice Vocabulary Word Search 1 Answer Key

Words are placed backwards, forward, diagonally, up and down. Clues listed below can help you find the words. Circle the hidden vocabulary words in the maze.

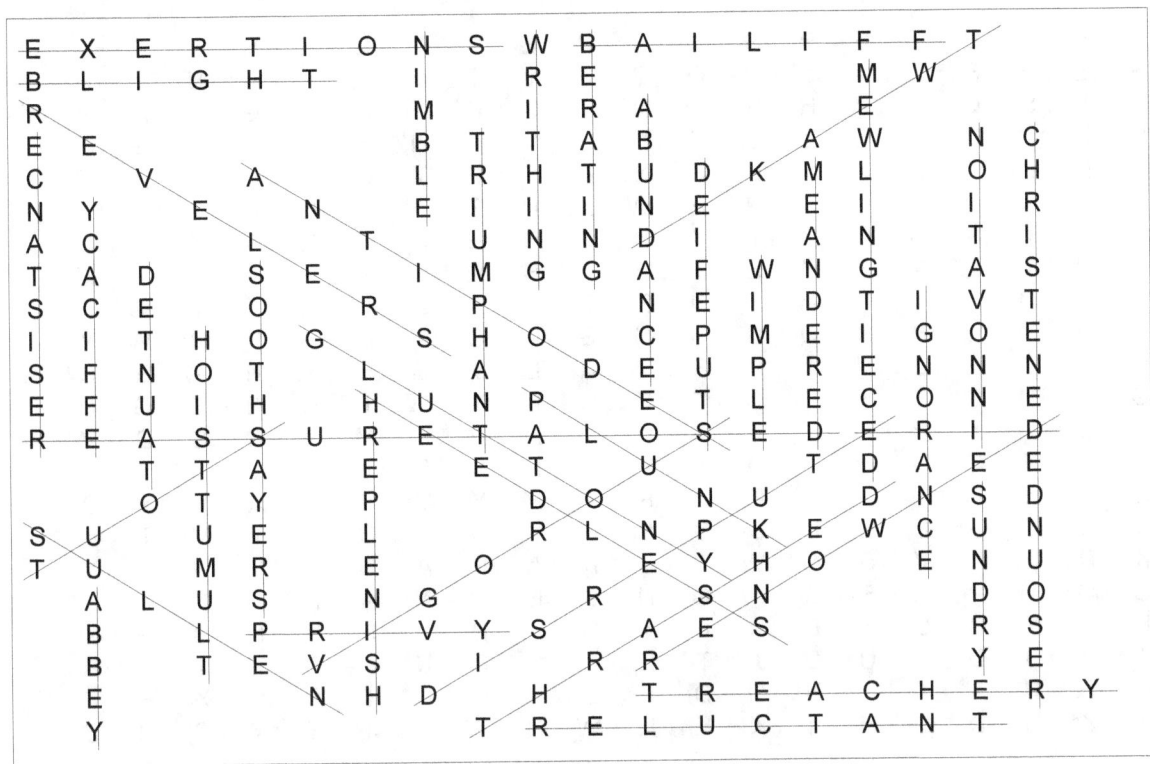

A sharp pull or twist (7)
An improvement (10)
An outhouse (5)
Arresting officer (7)
Astonished; shocked (9)
Betrayal; disloyalty (9)
Convent; monastery (5)
Curse (6)
Deserted; abandoned (8)
Dishonesty (6)
Dishonor (9)
Dreadful; awful (4)
Drinkers; carousers (8)
Echoed (9)
Effectiveness; capability (8)
Efforts; labors (9)
Encourage; inspire (8)
Energetic (8)
Excessive overeating (8)
Famous (8)
Heavy set (5)
Lift up (5)
Lively; quick (6)

Many; numerous (6)
Mocked; sneered (7)
Named (10)
Opposition (10)
Plenty (9)
Prophets; fortunetellers (11)
Rambled (9)
Restock (9)
Scolding (8)
Silent (6)
Spirit; spunk (5)
Tossed violently about (8)
Turmoil (6)
Turning and twisting from pain (8)
Unawareness; inexperience (9)
Uninhabited islands S. E. of New Zealand (9)
Unmindful (8)
Unwilling (9)
Victorious (10)
Whimpering; whining (7)
Woman's headcloth drawn in folds about the chin (6)

Midwife's Apprentice Vocabulary Word Search 2

Words are placed backwards, forward, diagonally, up and down. Clues listed below can help you find the words. Circle the hidden vocabulary words in the maze.

```
R E V E L E R S T U P E F I E D H T B G
E E R S S U O R G I V T L Q P A U L K
L T S O U U H S I N E L P E R U G M I P
U H G O R N L G E L B M I N N P G U G J
C R L T U F D L F N I F E T Q Y L L H X
T A U H P N B R E W N R E A D G I T T M
A S T S G H D T Y N P D E E N H N X S C
N H T A N N H E F P A B K N T D G X L M
T E O Y I C W Z D F T A T Z O R E Y W R
I D N E H H Q D C H E I C M B W I R W Y
P P Y R S H J P B W R L J C S Y N W E H
O R M S E E P G T C N I Y W T H N E G D
D O M X R E B T G O F M I M B O S D V
E S R G H D T D T V S F N E T X V M T F
S P X W T L A F I R T M Y V W Y A V Y B
Q E X S C E L B S S E W N T C L T V T L
K R I K V S O W T L R A I A D E I N C Y
C O M P A S S I O N S E C N A R O N G I
H U Y B L J E S U T C I P H P I N S G X
J S B D Z U D J T E F B F U E D Z J R R
B E R A T I N G D F S N O I T R E X E F
Y Z N D L H B K E R W G W F J E Y C N C
```

A sharp pull or twist (7)
An improvement (10)
An outhouse (5)
Arresting officer (7)
Astonished; shocked (9)
Bartering; dickering (8)
Beating grain to separate seeds from stalk (9)
Betrayal; disloyalty (9)
Convent; monastery (5)
Curse (6)
Deserted; abandoned (8)
Dishonesty (6)
Dishonor (9)
Dreadful; awful (4)
Drinkers; carousers (8)
Echoed (9)
Effectiveness; capability (8)
Efforts; labors (9)
Energetic (8)
Excessive overeating (8)
Famous (8)
Heavy set (5)
Lift up (5)

Lively; quick (6)
Many; numerous (6)
Mocked; sneered (7)
Parts of the Lord's Prayer (12)
Prophets; fortunetellers (11)
Rambled (9)
Restock (9)
Scolding (8)
Seriousness (9)
Silent (6)
Spirit; spunk (5)
Sympathy; caring (10)
Tossed violently about (8)
Turmoil (6)
Unawareness; inexperience (9)
Uninhabited islands S. E. of New Zealand (9)
Unmindful (8)
Unwilling (9)
Well-to-do (10)
Whimpering; whining (7)
Woman's headcloth drawn in folds about the chin (6)

Midwife's Apprentice Vocabulary Word Search 2 Answer Key

Words are placed backwards, forward, diagonally, up and down. Clues listed below can help you find the words. Circle the hidden vocabulary words in the maze.

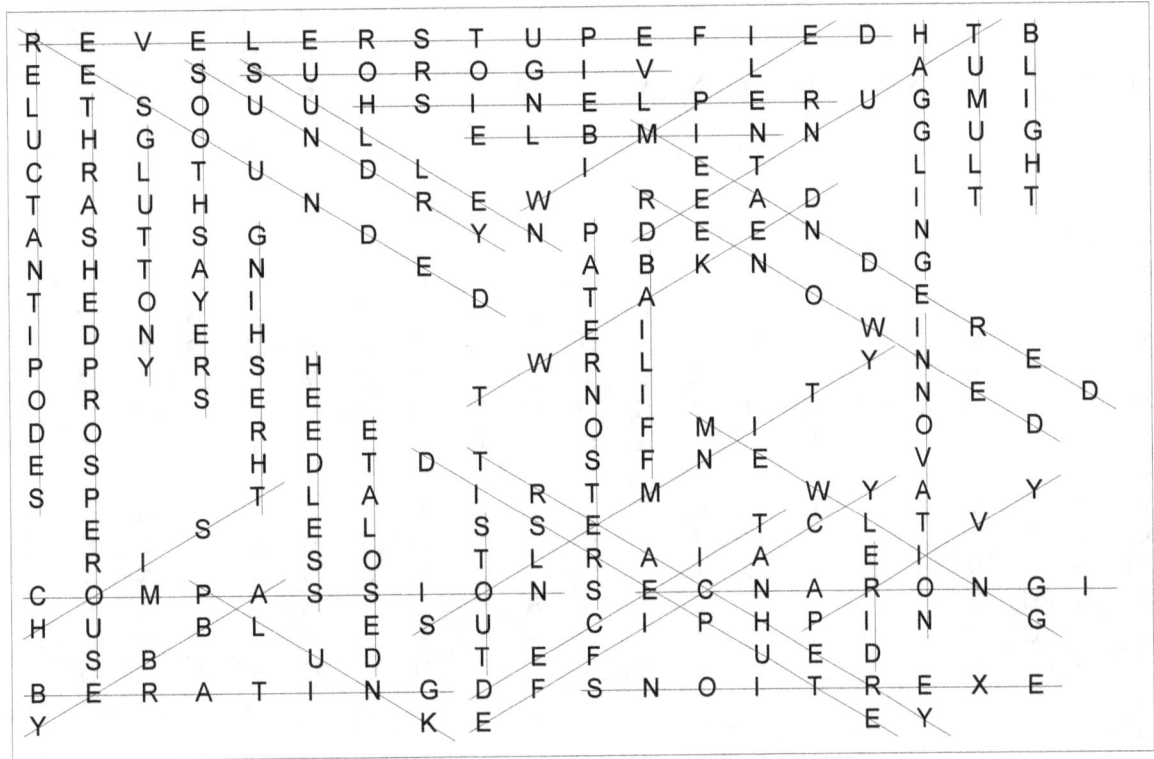

A sharp pull or twist (7)
An improvement (10)
An outhouse (5)
Arresting officer (7)
Astonished; shocked (9)
Bartering; dickering (8)
Beating grain to separate seeds from stalk (9)
Betrayal; disloyalty (9)
Convent; monastery (5)
Curse (6)
Deserted; abandoned (8)
Dishonesty (6)
Dishonor (9)
Dreadful; awful (4)
Drinkers; carousers (8)
Echoed (9)
Effectiveness; capability (8)
Efforts; labors (9)
Energetic (8)
Excessive overeating (8)
Famous (8)
Heavy set (5)
Lift up (5)

Lively; quick (6)
Many; numerous (6)
Mocked; sneered (7)
Parts of the Lord's Prayer (12)
Prophets; fortunetellers (11)
Rambled (9)
Restock (9)
Scolding (8)
Seriousness (9)
Silent (6)
Spirit; spunk (5)
Sympathy; caring (10)
Tossed violently about (8)
Turmoil (6)
Unawareness; inexperience (9)
Uninhabited islands S. E. of New Zealand (9)
Unmindful (8)
Unwilling (9)
Well-to-do (10)
Whimpering; whining (7)
Woman's headcloth drawn in folds about the chin (6)

Midwife's Apprentice Vocabulary Word Search 3

```
V I G O R O U S R E T S O N R E T A P W
T T N S M X H O F C S H V S A B R H
U R I T O W S R L F E K M Z U U O W
M I L O O B A T S E I W R T N P G
U U G U R C N N U F M K A D X E N
L M G T M S J M L P E A A E D R
T P A E E F W E L D E Z I E C D N Z
W H H R N A S J E G S F M T W P M
E A Y U T Y S C R N U X G I M Y L R X
A N N S I E I O T Z N U E Y D O V
K T O S N R D H I L T I P O D E I D
E F T A G S T R J L D K T W S G N G
D V T E P I O N S D N A C X S O C W
J W U R R T T Q E Y P R Y G Y L G G
R V L W C Z S D P C M H E N D H A Z D
R E G I Z C I M W E S D B J V D T I Q Z
E Y V I R P O B A I L I F F E X E H Y N
N N M E D C H G N T M V B H J L B S R N
O R P M L K S E R Z C P S L B B B E D S
W P L R N E L N W F V A M I B Y R N N
N D U Z D P R L Y Y R S E A G B T U N
E J C C E M R S Z H J N S H H H S L
D Q K R D I R E T N A T C U L E R T H Q
```

ABBEY
ABUNDANCE
ANTIPODES
BAILIFF
BERATING
BLIGHT
COMPENDIUM
DECEIT
DESOLATE
DIRE
EFFICACY
FERMENTING
GLUTTONY
HAGGLING
HEEDLESS

HOIST
MEANDERED
MEWLING
NIMBLE
PATERNOSTERS
PLUCK
PRIVY
PROSPEROUS
REASSURE
RELUCTANT
RENOWNED
REPLENISH
REVELERS
SOLEMNITY
SOOTHSAYERS

STOUT
STUPEFIED
SULLEN
SUNDRY
TAUNTED
THRASHED
THRESHING
TREACHERY
TRIUMPHANT
TUMULT
TWEAKED
VICTORIOUS
VIGOROUS
WIMPLE
WRITHING

Midwife's Apprentice Vocabulary Word Search 3 Answer Key

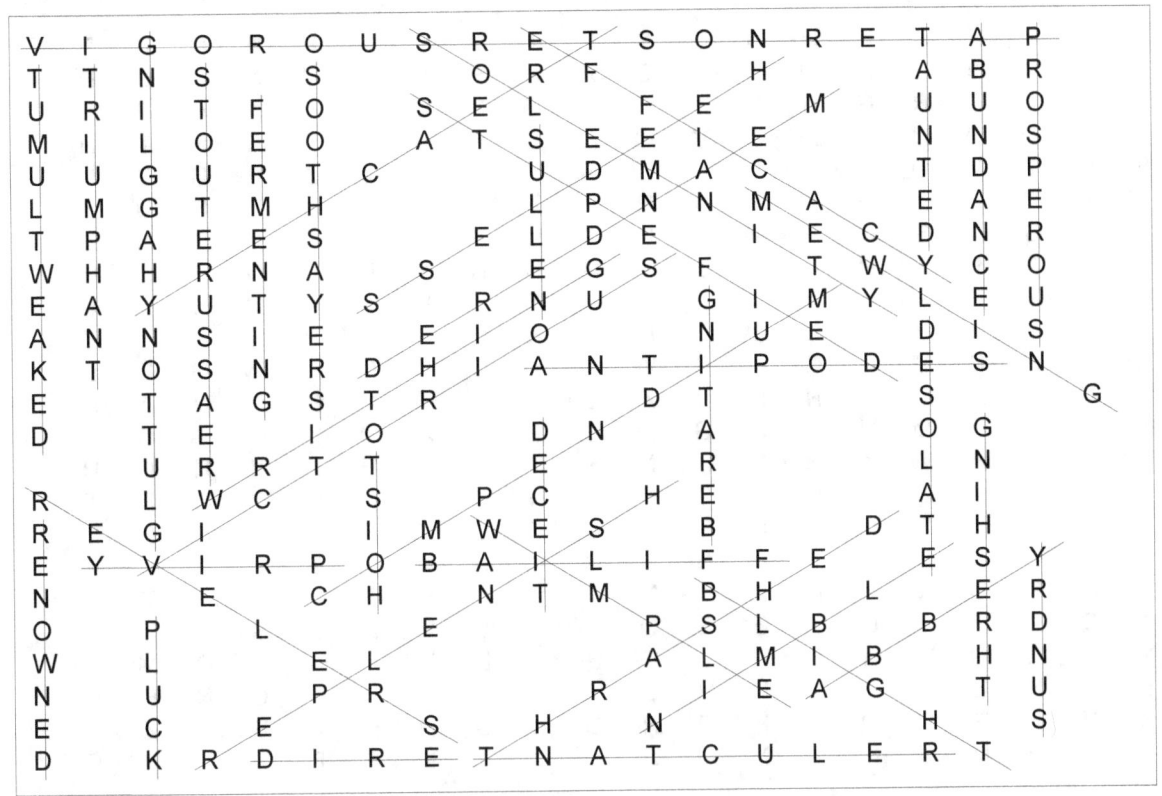

ABBEY	HOIST	STOUT
ABUNDANCE	MEANDERED	STUPEFIED
ANTIPODES	MEWLING	SULLEN
BAILIFF	NIMBLE	SUNDRY
BERATING	PATERNOSTERS	TAUNTED
BLIGHT	PLUCK	THRASHED
COMPENDIUM	PRIVY	THRESHING
DECEIT	PROSPEROUS	TREACHERY
DESOLATE	REASSURE	TRIUMPHANT
DIRE	RELUCTANT	TUMULT
EFFICACY	RENOWNED	TWEAKED
FERMENTING	REPLENISH	VICTORIOUS
GLUTTONY	REVELERS	VIGOROUS
HAGGLING	SOLEMNITY	WIMPLE
HEEDLESS	SOOTHSAYERS	WRITHING

Midwife's Apprentice Vocabulary Word Search 4

```
R W R I T H I N G Y E T W E A K E D K P
E V S N D S M H N S X R S O U N D E D
S I O C R G U N J U E G E V C L L K S
I G O O N S I Z V O R L U T Z A R H
S O T M O E D T X I T Y U V P B S C
T R H P I D N V A R I X E R T D X U Z
A O S E S O E M J U O H E D P T M F N Z
N U A T S P P S B X N D Y I D O B D N
C S Y E A I M U O U S T L W Y R M N R G
E T E N P T O L Q T R E A C H E W R Y Z
Q O R C M N C L C W A S D G C W G C L
S U S E O A N E B Z B T S R N B L N A F
S T A N C H I N G M D T E A D L I I C J
P L U R W K H N I N S P D E E I N G H
R M Y P Z X I N O I L N G S C G G S I H
I L E X E L J I O E U W G Y E H W E F T
V Z B A G F T H N B O W C N I T A R D B
Y Z B G N A I I A N A C I F T M F H E H
J Q A V V D S E E Q D I S M Z S S T K P
Y H R O V H E R D W B L H P A Y C M Y
D E N E T S I R H C Y Q P I R L U N F D
X N H P R O S P E R O U S H F L E V Z X
I T U M U L T N G D L V T L P F N P N F
```

ABBEY
ABUNDANCE
ANTIPODES
BAILIFF
BERATING
BLIGHT
CHRISTENED
COMPASSION
COMPENDIUM
DECEIT
DESOLATE
DIRE
EFFICACY
EXERTIONS
GLUTTONY
HAGGLING
HEEDLESS
HOIST
INCOMPETENCE
INNOVATION
LUXURIOUS
MEANDERED
MEWLING
NIMBLE
PLUCK
PRIVY
PROSPEROUS
RELUCTANT
RENOWNED
REPLENISH
RESISTANCE
RESOUNDED
REVELERS
SOOTHSAYERS
STANCHING
STOUT
STUPEFIED
SULLEN
SUNDRY
TAUNTED
THRASHED
THRESHING
TREACHERY
TUMULT
TWEAKED
VIGOROUS
WIMPLE
WRITHING

Midwife's Apprentice Vocabulary Word Search 4 Answer Key

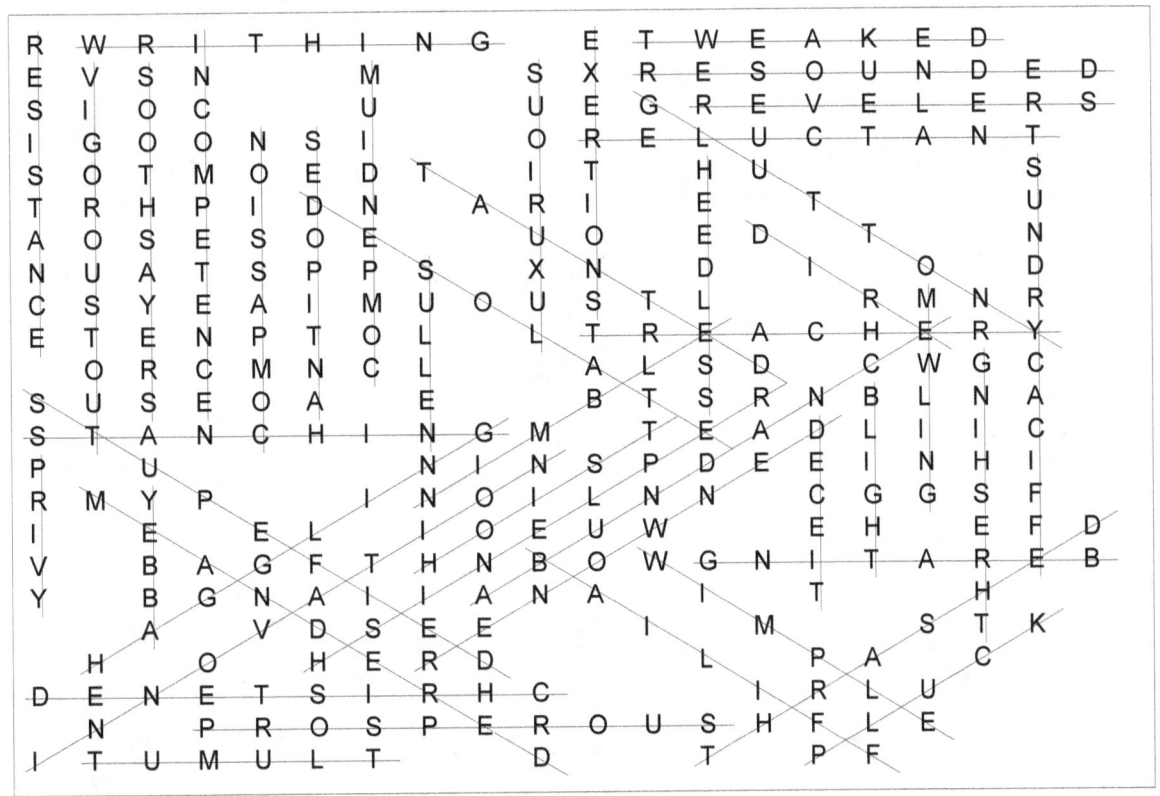

ABBEY	HEEDLESS	REVELERS
ABUNDANCE	HOIST	SOOTHSAYERS
ANTIPODES	INCOMPETENCE	STANCHING
BAILIFF	INNOVATION	STOUT
BERATING	LUXURIOUS	STUPEFIED
BLIGHT	MEANDERED	SULLEN
CHRISTENED	MEWLING	SUNDRY
COMPASSION	NIMBLE	TAUNTED
COMPENDIUM	PLUCK	THRASHED
DECEIT	PRIVY	THRESHING
DESOLATE	PROSPEROUS	TREACHERY
DIRE	RELUCTANT	TUMULT
EFFICACY	RENOWNED	TWEAKED
EXERTIONS	REPLENISH	VIGOROUS
GLUTTONY	RESISTANCE	WIMPLE
HAGGLING	RESOUNDED	WRITHING

Midwife's Apprentice Vocabulary Crossword 1

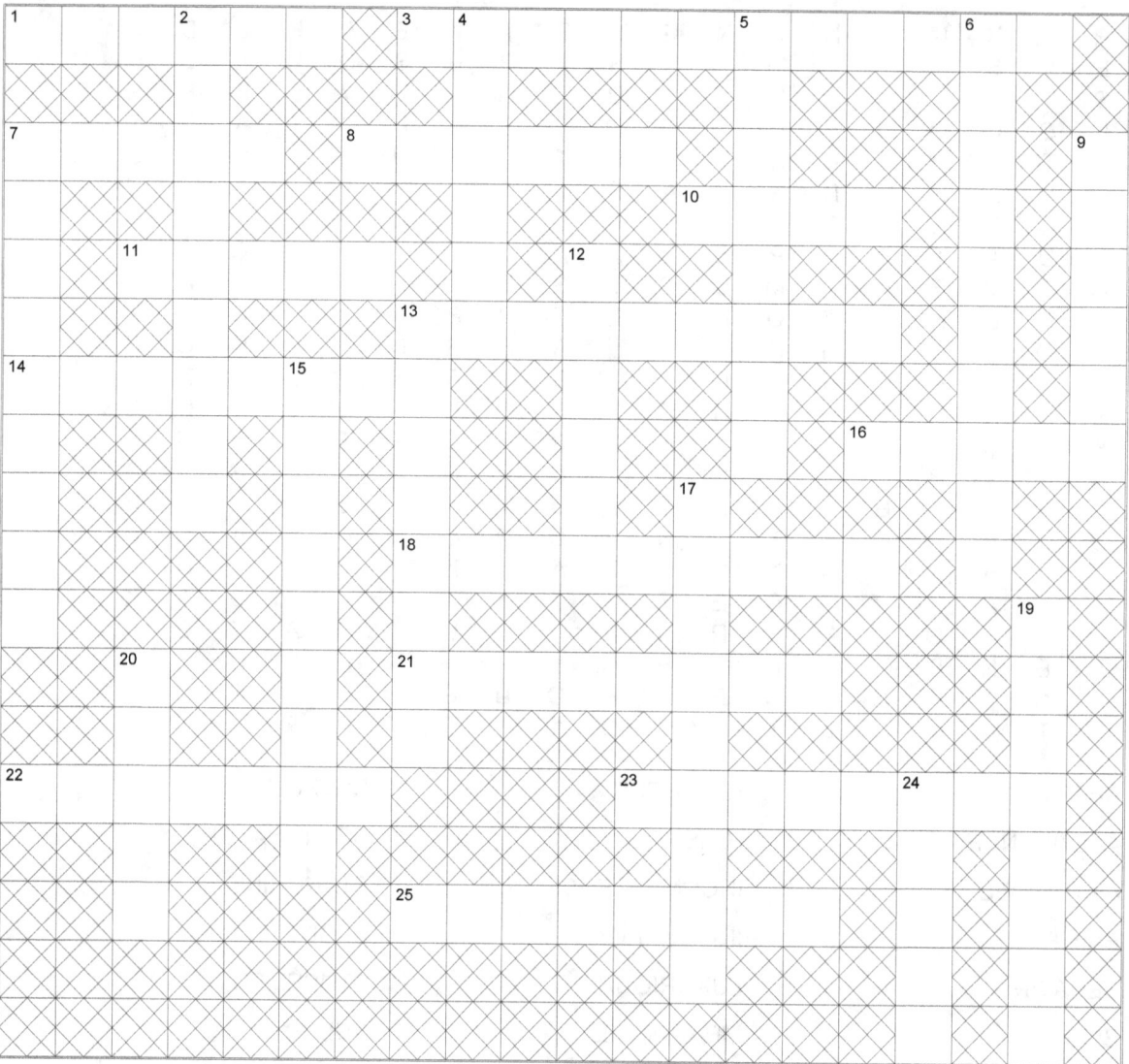

Across
1. Dishonesty
3. Stupidity; inability
7. Convent; monastery
8. Turmoil
10. Dreadful; awful
11. Heavy set
13. Unwilling
14. Deserted; abandoned
16. An outhouse
18. Stopping the flow
21. Drinkers; carousers
22. Mocked; sneered
23. Tossed violently about
25. Famous

Down
2. Efforts; labors
4. Lively; quick
5. Effectiveness; capability
6. Sympathy; caring
7. Plenty
9. Many; numerous
12. Silent
13. Encourage; inspire
15. Uninhabited islands S. E. of New Zealand
17. Beating grain to separate seeds from stalk
19. Unmindful
20. Spirit; spunk
24. Lift up

Midwife's Apprentice Vocabulary Crossword 1 Answer Key

[Crossword grid with answers:
1A DECEIT, 3A INCOMPETENCE, 7A ABBEY, 8A TUMULT, 10A DIRE, 11A STOUT, 13A RELUCTANT, 14A DESOLATE, 16A PRIVY, 18A STANCHING, 21A REVELERS, 22A TAUNTED, 23A THRASHED, 25A RENOWNED
2D EXERTIONS, 4D NIMBLE, 5D EFFICACY, 6D COMPASSION, 7D ABUNDANCE, 9D SUNDRY, 12D SILENCE, 13D REASSURE, 15D ANTIPODES, 17D THRASHING, 19D HEEDLESS, 20D PLUCK, 24D HOIST]

Across
1. Dishonesty
3. Stupidity; inability
7. Convent; monastery
8. Turmoil
10. Dreadful; awful
11. Heavy set
13. Unwilling
14. Deserted; abandoned
16. An outhouse
18. Stopping the flow
21. Drinkers; carousers
22. Mocked; sneered
23. Tossed violently about
25. Famous

Down
2. Efforts; labors
4. Lively; quick
5. Effectiveness; capability
6. Sympathy; caring
7. Plenty
9. Many; numerous
12. Silent
13. Encourage; inspire
15. Uninhabited islands S. E. of New Zealand
17. Beating grain to separate seeds from stalk
19. Unmindful
20. Spirit; spunk
24. Lift up

Midwife's Apprentice Vocabulary Crossword 2

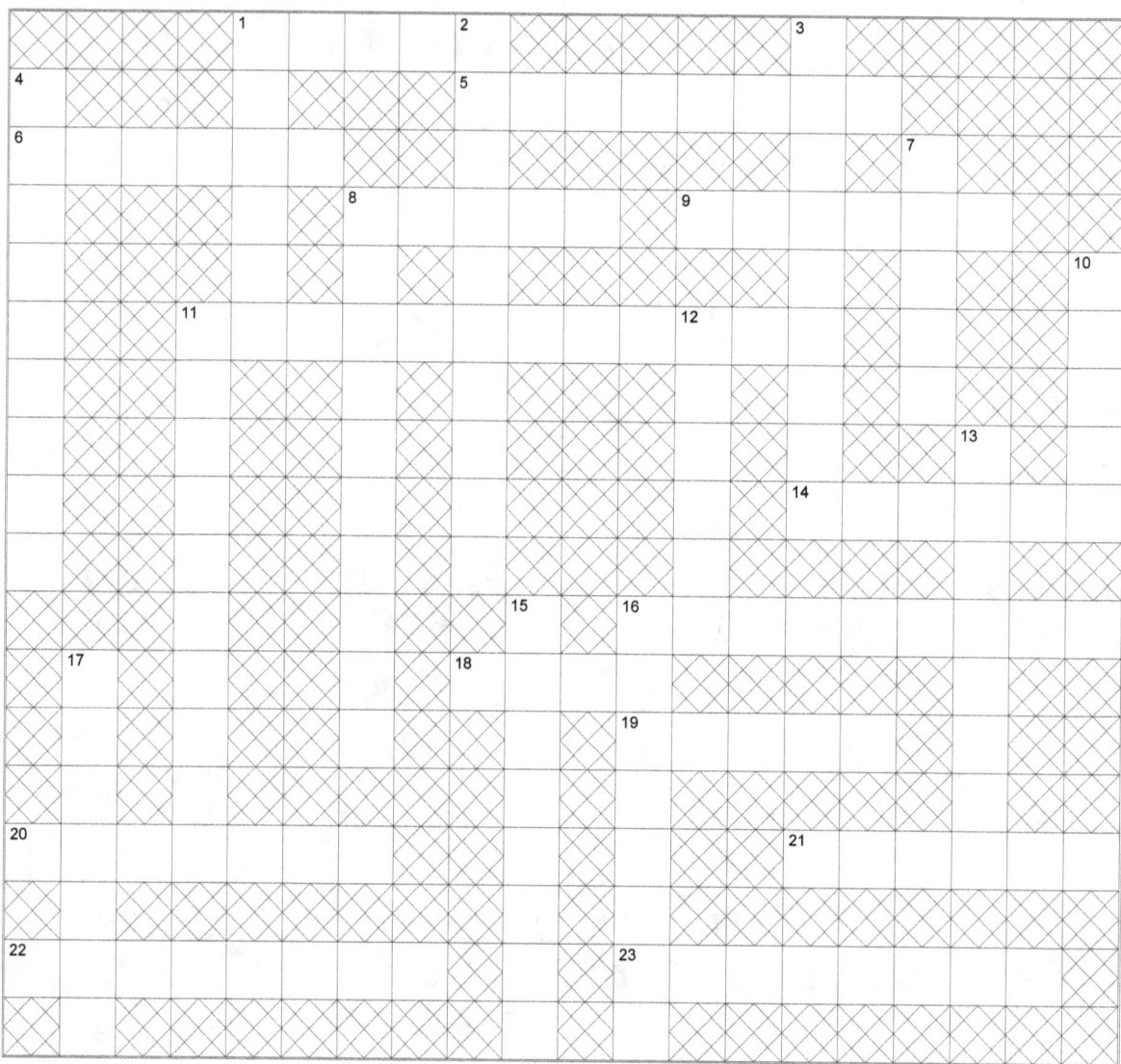

Across
1. Heavy set
5. Famous
6. Turmoil
8. Spirit; spunk
9. Many; numerous
11. Stupidity; inability
14. Dishonesty
16. Unwilling
18. Dreadful; awful
19. Convent; monastery
20. Mocked; sneered
21. Curse
22. Deserted; abandoned
23. Drinkers; carousers

Down
1. Silent
2. Victorious
3. Rambled
4. Astonished; shocked
7. An outhouse
8. Well-to-do
10. Lift up
11. An improvement
12. Lively; quick
13. Scolding
15. Energetic
16. Encourage; inspire
17. A sharp pull or twist

Midwife's Apprentice Vocabulary Crossword 2 Answer Key

Across
1. Heavy set
5. Famous
6. Turmoil
8. Spirit; spunk
9. Many; numerous
11. Stupidity; inability
14. Dishonesty
16. Unwilling
18. Dreadful; awful
19. Convent; monastery
20. Mocked; sneered
21. Curse
22. Deserted; abandoned
23. Drinkers; carousers

Down
1. Silent
2. Victorious
3. Rambled
4. Astonished; shocked
7. An outhouse
8. Well-to-do
10. Lift up
11. An improvement
12. Lively; quick
13. Scolding
15. Energetic
16. Encourage; inspire
17. A sharp pull or twist

Midwife's Apprentice Vocabulary Crossword 3

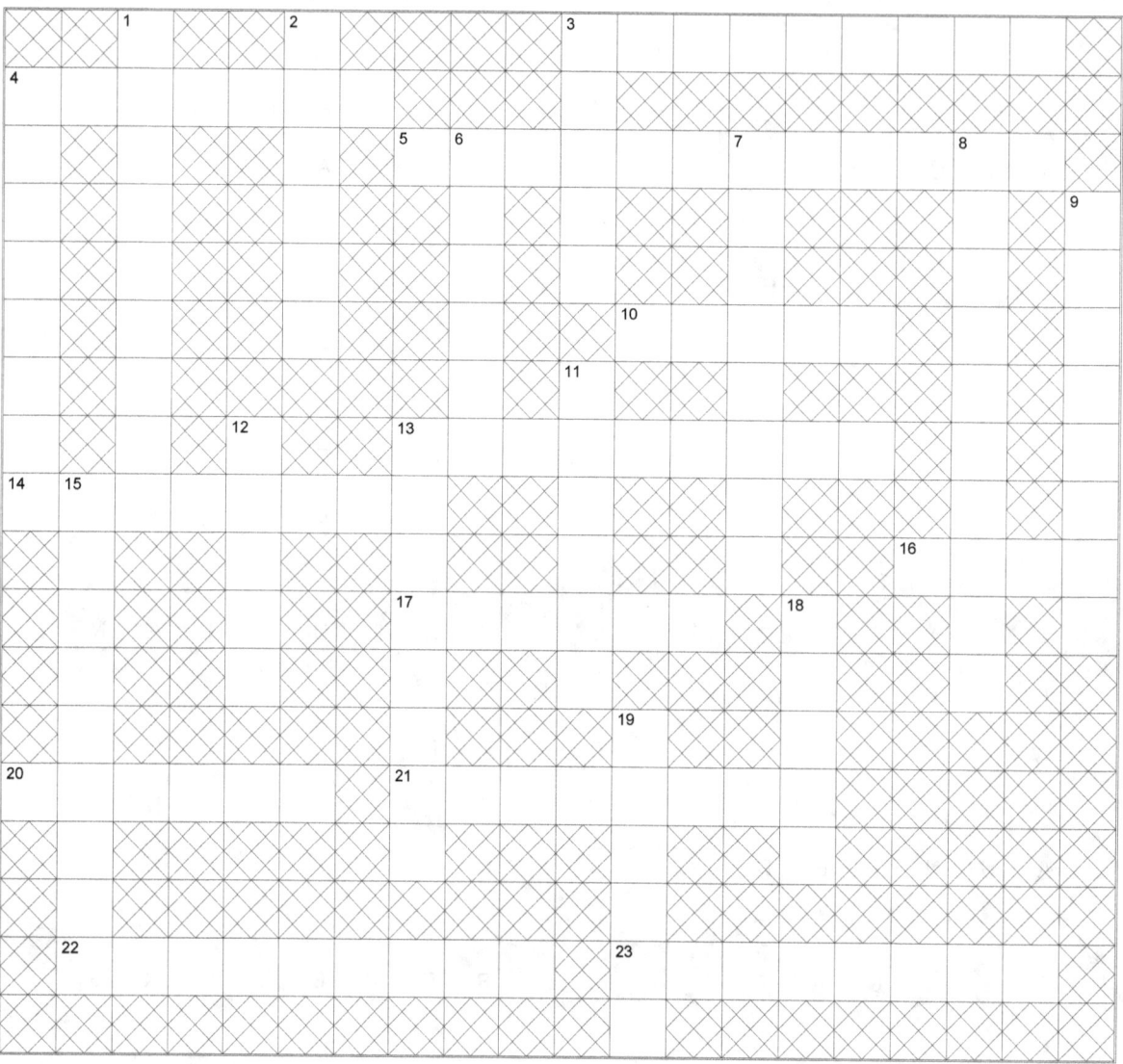

Across
3. Astonished; shocked
4. Mocked; sneered
5. Stupidity; inability
10. An outhouse
13. Unwilling
14. Deserted; abandoned
16. Dreadful; awful
17. Silent
20. Woman's headcloth drawn in folds about the chin
21. Drinkers; carousers
22. Stopping the flow
23. Bartering; dickering

Down
1. Rich; fine
2. Dishonesty
3. Heavy set
4. Tossed violently about
6. Lively; quick
7. Effectiveness; capability
8. Sympathy; caring
9. Famous
11. Turmoil
12. Spirit; spunk
13. Encourage; inspire
15. Efforts; labors
18. Lift up
19. Curse

Midwife's Apprentice Vocabulary Crossword 3 Answer Key

Across
- 3. Astonished; shocked
- 4. Mocked; sneered
- 5. Stupidity; inability
- 10. An outhouse
- 13. Unwilling
- 14. Deserted; abandoned
- 16. Dreadful; awful
- 17. Silent
- 20. Woman's headcloth drawn in folds about the chin
- 21. Drinkers; carousers
- 22. Stopping the flow
- 23. Bartering; dickering

Down
- 1. Rich; fine
- 2. Dishonesty
- 3. Heavy set
- 4. Tossed violently about
- 6. Lively; quick
- 7. Effectiveness; capability
- 8. Sympathy; caring
- 9. Famous
- 11. Turmoil
- 12. Spirit; spunk
- 13. Encourage; inspire
- 15. Efforts; labors
- 18. Lift up
- 19. Curse

Midwife's Apprentice Vocabulary Crossword 4

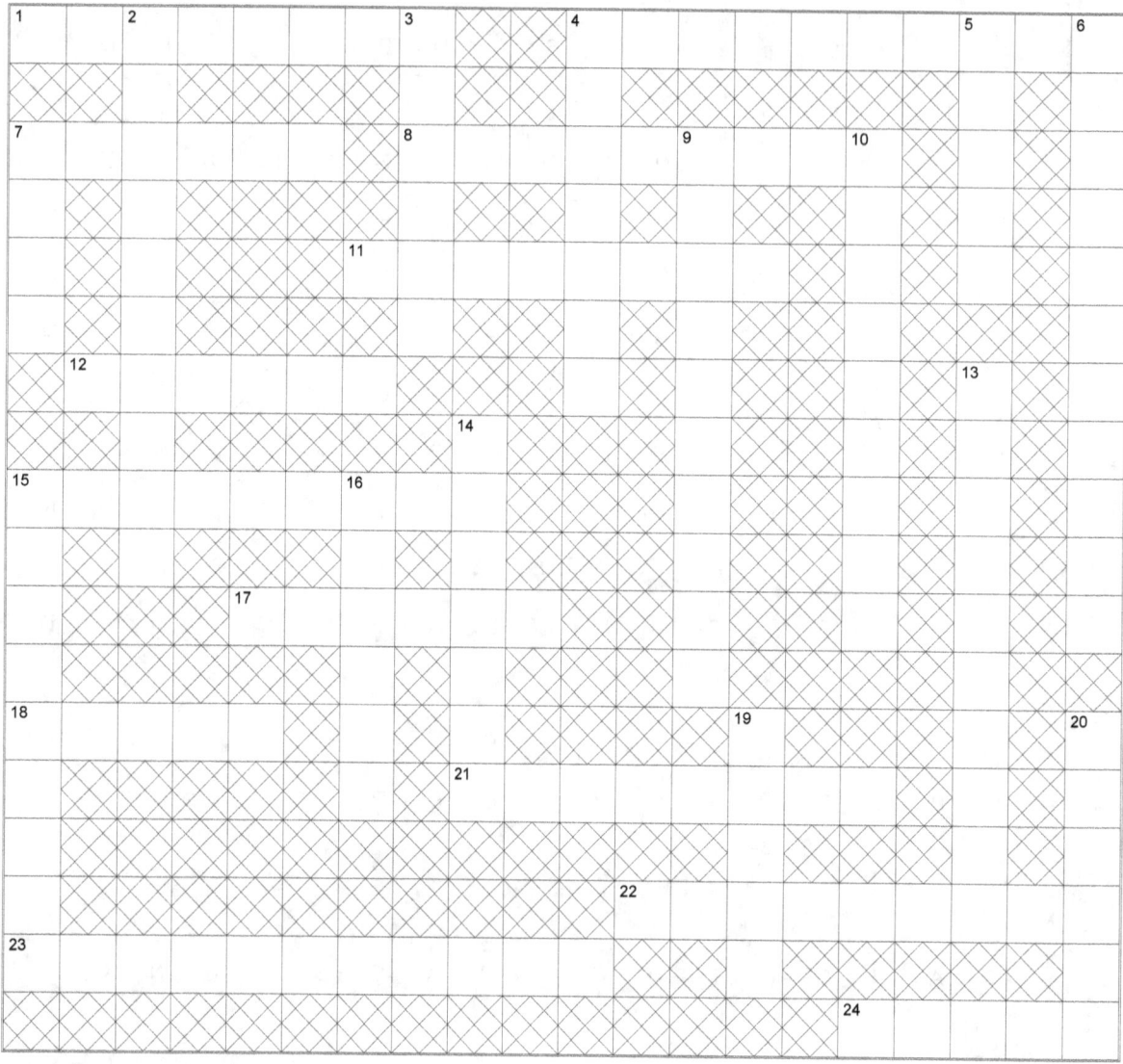

Across
1. Drinkers; carousers
4. Victorious
7. Dishonesty
8. Rich; fine
11. Scolding
12. Woman's headcloth drawn in folds about the chin
15. Plenty
17. Turmoil
18. Spirit; spunk
21. Excessive overeating
22. Echoed
23. Prophets; fortunetellers
24. An outhouse

Down
2. Successful
3. Silent
4. Mocked; sneered
5. Convent; monastery
6. Fascinating
7. Dreadful; awful
9. An improvement
10. Stopping the flow
13. Named
14. Whimpering; whining
15. Uninhabited islands S. E. of New Zealand
16. Lively; quick
19. Lift up
20. Many; numerous

Midwife's Apprentice Vocabulary Crossword 4 Answer Key

Across
1. Drinkers; carousers
4. Victorious
7. Dishonesty
8. Rich; fine
11. Scolding
12. Woman's headcloth drawn in folds about the chin
15. Plenty
17. Turmoil
18. Spirit; spunk
21. Excessive overeating
22. Echoed
23. Prophets; fortunetellers
24. An outhouse

Down
2. Successful
3. Silent
4. Mocked; sneered
5. Convent; monastery
6. Fascinating
7. Dreadful; awful
9. An improvement
10. Stopping the flow
13. Named
14. Whimpering; whining
15. Uninhabited islands S. E. of New Zealand
16. Lively; quick
19. Lift up
20. Many; numerous

Midwife's Apprentice Vocabulary Juggle Letters 1

1. BBYEA = 1. _____
   Convent; monastery

2. UTUTML = 2. _____
   Turmoil

3. NBEAUNCAD = 3. _____
   Plenty

4. KULCP = 4. _____
   Spirit; spunk

5. ETRUNLCAT = 5. _____
   Unwilling

6. NIGMLEW = 6. _____
   Whimpering; whining

7. MOETNEIENCPC = 7. _____
   Stupidity; inability

8. GNNHCITAS = 8. _____
   Stopping the flow

9. DMECIUNPOM = 9. _____
   Comprehensive summary

10. VOOIITANNN =10. _____
    An improvement

11. DNSRYU =11. _____
    Many; numerous

12. ACEISTSREN =12. _____
    Opposition

13. DSEEHSEL =13. _____
    Unmindful

14. PAUNTTRIHM =14. _____
    Victorious

15. OEENFCRHHT =15. _____
    From now on

Midwife's Apprentice Vocabulary Juggle Letters 1 Answer Key

1. BBYEA = 1. ABBEY
Convent; monastery

2. UTUTML = 2. TUMULT
Turmoil

3. NBEAUNCAD = 3. ABUNDANCE
Plenty

4. KULCP = 4. PLUCK
Spirit; spunk

5. ETRUNLCAT = 5. RELUCTANT
Unwilling

6. NIGMLEW = 6. MEWLING
Whimpering; whining

7. MOETNEIENCPC = 7. INCOMPETENCE
Stupidity; inability

8. GNNHCITAS = 8. STANCHING
Stopping the flow

9. DMECIUNPOM = 9. COMPENDIUM
Comprehensive summary

10. VOOIITANNN =10. INNOVATION
An improvement

11. DNSRYU =11. SUNDRY
Many; numerous

12. ACEISTSREN =12. RESISTANCE
Opposition

13. DSEEHSEL =13. HEEDLESS
Unmindful

14. PAUNTTRIHM =14. TRIUMPHANT
Victorious

15. OEENFCRHHT =15. HENCEFORTH
From now on

Midwife's Apprentice Vocabulary Juggle Letters 2

1. FLIBFAI = 1. _____
Arresting officer

2. CSETARESNI = 2. _____
Opposition

3. ILIANGNTTAZ = 3. _____
Fascinating

4. DEHSEELS = 4. _____
Unmindful

5. DTRHEEISCN = 5. _____
Named

6. HTLIGB = 6. _____
Curse

7. HTIANGCNS = 7. _____
Stopping the flow

8. NGALGIHG = 8. _____
Bartering; dickering

9. VAONTNIONI = 9. _____
An improvement

10. NEEGTMFRNI =10. _____
Ripening

11. RTNEPSTSAERO =11. _____
Parts of the Lord's Prayer

12. LESADTOE =12. _____
Deserted; abandoned

13. ETADKEW =13. _____
A sharp pull or twist

14. EERONFHCTH =14. _____
From now on

15. SEOXIRTNE =15. _____
Efforts; labors

Midwife's Apprentice Vocabulary Juggle Letters 2 Answer Key

1. FLIBFAI = 1. BAILIFF
Arresting officer

2. CSETARESNI = 2. RESISTANCE
Opposition

3. ILIANGNTTAZ = 3. TANTALIZING
Fascinating

4. DEHSEELS = 4. HEEDLESS
Unmindful

5. DTRHEEISCN = 5. CHRISTENED
Named

6. HTLIGB = 6. BLIGHT
Curse

7. HTIANGCNS = 7. STANCHING
Stopping the flow

8. NGALGIHG = 8. HAGGLING
Bartering; dickering

9. VAONTNIONI = 9. INNOVATION
An improvement

10. NEEGTMFRNI =10. FERMENTING
Ripening

11. RTNEPSTSAERO =11. PATERNOSTERS
Parts of the Lord's Prayer

12. LESADTOE =12. DESOLATE
Deserted; abandoned

13. ETADKEW =13. TWEAKED
A sharp pull or twist

14. EERONFHCTH =14. HENCEFORTH
From now on

15. SEOXIRTNE =15. EXERTIONS
Efforts; labors

Midwife's Apprentice Vocabulary Juggle Letters 3

1. GSHTIEHRN = 1. _____
   Beating grain to separate seeds from stalk

2. IHRNLSEPE = 2. _____
   Restock

3. ORVSIUGO = 3. _____
   Energetic

4. IOCIVSRTOU = 4. _____
   Successful

5. UMTLTU = 5. _____
   Turmoil

6. OEELDAST = 6. _____
   Deserted; abandoned

7. IAITANTZNLG = 7. _____
   Fascinating

8. IPEMWL = 8. _____
   Woman's headcloth drawn in folds about the chin

9. EFTHCEHONR = 9. _____
   From now on

10. IFLFIAB = 10. _____
    Arresting officer

11. OSSYTAHSREO = 11. _____
    Prophets; fortunetellers

12. TFMGNEIENR = 12. _____
    Ripening

13. ANCOINRGE = 13. _____
    Unawareness; inexperience

14. TSUOT = 14. _____
    Heavy set

15. RRECYAHTE = 15. _____
    Betrayal; disloyalty

Midwife's Apprentice Vocabulary Juggle Letters 3 Answer Key

1. GSHTIEHRN = 1. THRESHING
   Beating grain to separate seeds from stalk

2. IHRNLSEPE = 2. REPLENISH
   Restock

3. ORVSIUGO = 3. VIGOROUS
   Energetic

4. IOCIVSRTOU = 4. VICTORIOUS
   Successful

5. UMTLTU = 5. TUMULT
   Turmoil

6. OEELDAST = 6. DESOLATE
   Deserted; abandoned

7. IAITANTZNLG = 7. TANTALIZING
   Fascinating

8. IPEMWL = 8. WIMPLE
   Woman's headcloth drawn in folds about the chin

9. EFTHCEHONR = 9. HENCEFORTH
   From now on

10. IFLFIAB = 10. BAILIFF
    Arresting officer

11. OSSYTAHSREO = 11. SOOTHSAYERS
    Prophets; fortunetellers

12. TFMGNEIENR = 12. FERMENTING
    Ripening

13. ANCOINRGE = 13. IGNORANCE
    Unawareness; inexperience

14. TSUOT = 14. STOUT
    Heavy set

15. RRECYAHTE = 15. TREACHERY
    Betrayal; disloyalty

Midwife's Apprentice Vocabulary Juggle Letters 4

1. SLROUIUXU = 1. _____
   Rich; fine

2. YUNSRD = 2. _____
   Many; numerous

3. ELSTEDAO = 3. _____
   Deserted; abandoned

4. TSORTANEERPS = 4. _____
   Parts of the Lord's Prayer

5. FEEPSTIDU = 5. _____
   Astonished; shocked

6. VPYIR = 6. _____
   An outhouse

7. LGWIMEN = 7. _____
   Whimpering; whining

8. SEHEDELS = 8. _____
   Unmindful

9. RGIIHWTN = 9. _____
   Turning and twisting from pain

10. DRIE =10. _____
    Dreadful; awful

11. SSTEYSAOHRO =11. _____
    Prophets; fortunetellers

12. DEABANUCN =12. _____
    Plenty

13. TSENEIXRO =13. _____
    Efforts; labors

14. LENULS =14. _____
    Silent

15. GNTSNCHIA =15. _____
    Stopping the flow

Midwife's Apprentice Vocabulary Juggle Letters 4 Answer Key

1. SLROUIUXU = 1. LUXURIOUS
   Rich; fine

2. YUNSRD = 2. SUNDRY
   Many; numerous

3. ELSTEDAO = 3. DESOLATE
   Deserted; abandoned

4. TSORTANEERPS = 4. PATERNOSTERS
   Parts of the Lord's Prayer

5. FEEPSTIDU = 5. STUPEFIED
   Astonished; shocked

6. VPYIR = 6. PRIVY
   An outhouse

7. LGWIMEN = 7. MEWLING
   Whimpering; whining

8. SEHEDELS = 8. HEEDLESS
   Unmindful

9. RGIIHWTN = 9. WRITHING
   Turning and twisting from pain

10. DRIE = 10. DIRE
    Dreadful; awful

11. SSTEYSAOHRO = 11. SOOTHSAYERS
    Prophets; fortunetellers

12. DEABANUCN = 12. ABUNDANCE
    Plenty

13. TSENEIXRO = 13. EXERTIONS
    Efforts; labors

14. LENULS = 14. SULLEN
    Silent

15. GNTSNCHIA = 15. STANCHING
    Stopping the flow

ABBEY	Convent; monastery
ABUNDANCE	Plenty
ANTIPODES	Uninhabited islands S. E. of New Zealand
BAILIFF	Arresting officer
BERATING	Scolding
BLIGHT	Curse

CHRISTENED	Named
COMPASSION	Sympathy; caring
COMPENDIUM	Comprehensive summary
DECEIT	Dishonesty
DESOLATE	Deserted; abandoned
DIRE	Dreadful; awful

DISREPUTE	Dishonor
EFFICACY	Effectiveness; capability
EXERTIONS	Efforts; labors
FERMENTING	Ripening
GLUTTONY	Excessive overeating
HAGGLING	Bartering; dickering

HEEDLESS	Unmindful
HENCEFORTH	From now on
HOIST	Lift up
IGNORANCE	Unawareness; inexperience
INCOMPETENCE	Stupidity; inability
INNOVATION	An improvement

LUXURIOUS	Rich; fine
MEANDERED	Rambled
MEWLING	Whimpering; whining
NIMBLE	Lively; quick
PATERNOSTERS	Parts of the Lord's Prayer
PLUCK	Spirit; spunk

PRIVY	An outhouse
PROSPEROUS	Well-to-do
REASSURE	Encourage; inspire
RELUCTANT	Unwilling
RENOWNED	Famous
REPLENISH	Restock

RESISTANCE	Opposition
RESOUNDED	Echoed
REVELERS	Drinkers; carousers
SOLEMNITY	Seriousness
SOOTHSAYERS	Prophets; fortunetellers
STANCHING	Stopping the flow

STOUT	Heavy set
STUPEFIED	Astonished; shocked
SULLEN	Silent
SUNDRY	Many; numerous
TANTALIZING	Fascinating
TAUNTED	Mocked; sneered

THRASHED	Tossed violently about
THRESHING	Beating grain to separate seeds from stalk
TREACHERY	Betrayal; disloyalty
TRIUMPHANT	Victorious
TUMULT	Turmoil
TWEAKED	A sharp pull or twist

VICTORIOUS	Successful
VIGOROUS	Energetic
WIMPLE	Woman's headcloth drawn in folds about the chin
WRITHING	Turning and twisting from pain

Midwife's Apprentice Vocabular

DESOLATE	EFFICACY	HAGGLING	SOLEMNITY	CHRISTENED
TANTALIZING	IGNORANCE	FERMENTING	HEEDLESS	RELUCTANT
BERATING	DECEIT	FREE SPACE	SUNDRY	RESOUNDED
ANTIPODES	MEWLING	DISREPUTE	TRIUMPHANT	TWEAKED
PLUCK	COMPENDIUM	STUPEFIED	WRITHING	STANCHING

Midwife's Apprentice Vocabular

ABUNDANCE	SOOTHSAYERS	BAILIFF	STOUT	HOIST
PRIVY	EXERTIONS	TAUNTED	THRESHING	REPLENISH
LUXURIOUS	REVELERS	FREE SPACE	VIGOROUS	MEANDERED
GLUTTONY	INNOVATION	TUMULT	REASSURE	PATERNOSTERS
RESISTANCE	TREACHERY	THRASHED	PROSPEROUS	HENCEFORTH

Midwife's Apprentice Vocabular

BAILIFF	FERMENTING	RESOUNDED	DISREPUTE	SOOTHSAYERS
MEANDERED	BERATING	TREACHERY	TRIUMPHANT	DECEIT
PATERNOSTERS	REASSURE	FREE SPACE	MEWLING	SOLEMNITY
HEEDLESS	COMPENDIUM	RESISTANCE	ANTIPODES	THRESHING
PRIVY	TUMULT	SUNDRY	COMPASSION	STANCHING

Midwife's Apprentice Vocabular

INCOMPETENCE	IGNORANCE	REVELERS	ABUNDANCE	REPLENISH
WIMPLE	RENOWNED	TAUNTED	PROSPEROUS	NIMBLE
RELUCTANT	VICTORIOUS	FREE SPACE	STOUT	HENCEFORTH
HOIST	DIRE	EXERTIONS	GLUTTONY	LUXURIOUS
ABBEY	CHRISTENED	WRITHING	SULLEN	TWEAKED

Midwife's Apprentice Vocabular

TUMULT	RENOWNED	INCOMPETENCE	STUPEFIED	TRIUMPHANT
CHRISTENED	RESOUNDED	STANCHING	THRESHING	TANTALIZING
WRITHING	DIRE	FREE SPACE	MEWLING	RELUCTANT
MEANDERED	COMPENDIUM	SOOTHSAYERS	TWEAKED	BAILIFF
PRIVY	ANTIPODES	LUXURIOUS	HEEDLESS	COMPASSION

Midwife's Apprentice Vocabular

STOUT	REPLENISH	VIGOROUS	SULLEN	PROSPEROUS
PATERNOSTERS	ABUNDANCE	DISREPUTE	SUNDRY	HENCEFORTH
DECEIT	BERATING	FREE SPACE	VICTORIOUS	THRASHED
HOIST	GLUTTONY	REASSURE	ABBEY	INNOVATION
BLIGHT	PLUCK	RESISTANCE	FERMENTING	DESOLATE

Midwife's Apprentice Vocabular

SUNDRY	EFFICACY	BERATING	GLUTTONY	HAGGLING
COMPENDIUM	STUPEFIED	TWEAKED	DISREPUTE	DIRE
RESISTANCE	STOUT	FREE SPACE	TAUNTED	TREACHERY
STANCHING	DESOLATE	THRASHED	SOLEMNITY	REVELERS
PROSPEROUS	TRIUMPHANT	REASSURE	INCOMPETENCE	PATERNOSTERS

Midwife's Apprentice Vocabular

COMPASSION	TANTALIZING	LUXURIOUS	THRESHING	NIMBLE
IGNORANCE	ABUNDANCE	RESOUNDED	MEWLING	HOIST
VICTORIOUS	HENCEFORTH	FREE SPACE	DECEIT	BLIGHT
REPLENISH	MEANDERED	TUMULT	PRIVY	INNOVATION
CHRISTENED	FERMENTING	HEEDLESS	BAILIFF	ANTIPODES

Midwife's Apprentice Vocabular

STOUT	PRIVY	RESOUNDED	HEEDLESS	TREACHERY
EFFICACY	FERMENTING	VICTORIOUS	SOLEMNITY	GLUTTONY
PLUCK	NIMBLE	FREE SPACE	HENCEFORTH	TAUNTED
SOOTHSAYERS	TUMULT	TRIUMPHANT	EXERTIONS	DESOLATE
CHRISTENED	PATERNOSTERS	SULLEN	LUXURIOUS	TWEAKED

Midwife's Apprentice Vocabular

COMPASSION	DISREPUTE	RESISTANCE	RENOWNED	THRESHING
REVELERS	ABUNDANCE	INNOVATION	WIMPLE	STANCHING
THRASHED	COMPENDIUM	FREE SPACE	ANTIPODES	HAGGLING
REPLENISH	SUNDRY	BAILIFF	IGNORANCE	REASSURE
RELUCTANT	STUPEFIED	ABBEY	PROSPEROUS	INCOMPETENCE

Midwife's Apprentice Vocabular

ANTIPODES	PROSPEROUS	HENCEFORTH	HEEDLESS	STUPEFIED
PATERNOSTERS	RELUCTANT	BLIGHT	CHRISTENED	FERMENTING
PLUNK	HAGGLING	FREE SPACE	PRIVY	REASSURE
ABUNDANCE	EFFICACY	STOUT	DESOLATE	REPLENISH
MEWLING	VIGOROUS	TREACHERY	TRIUMPHANT	BAILIFF

Midwife's Apprentice Vocabular

GLUTTONY	RESISTANCE	THRASHED	SOOTHSAYERS	NIMBLE
HOIST	TWEAKED	ABBEY	SULLEN	INCOMPETENCE
EXERTIONS	REVELERS	FREE SPACE	TAUNTED	SUNDRY
MEANDERED	INNOVATION	DIRE	WRITHING	BERATING
DECEIT	VICTORIOUS	TUMULT	COMPENDIUM	LUXURIOUS

Midwife's Apprentice Vocabular

TAUNTED	TWEAKED	FERMENTING	HEEDLESS	RESISTANCE
SULLEN	HOIST	TUMULT	LUXURIOUS	GLUTTONY
TREACHERY	REPLENISH	FREE SPACE	IGNORANCE	THRESHING
PRIVY	PLUCK	RENOWNED	SOOTHSAYERS	EFFICACY
REASSURE	COMPASSION	RESOUNDED	INNOVATION	DISREPUTE

Midwife's Apprentice Vocabular

VICTORIOUS	TRIUMPHANT	DESOLATE	STUPEFIED	STOUT
ANTIPODES	STANCHING	PATERNOSTERS	BLIGHT	THRASHED
DIRE	DECEIT	FREE SPACE	BERATING	BAILIFF
TANTALIZING	WIMPLE	WRITHING	SUNDRY	CHRISTENED
SOLEMNITY	RELUCTANT	INCOMPETENCE	MEANDERED	REVELERS

Midwife's Apprentice Vocabular

WIMPLE	SOLEMNITY	TAUNTED	SOOTHSAYERS	HENCEFORTH
HAGGLING	BLIGHT	SUNDRY	COMPENDIUM	RESOUNDED
DISREPUTE	VICTORIOUS	FREE SPACE	ABUNDANCE	TREACHERY
INNOVATION	EFFICACY	THRASHED	NIMBLE	ABBEY
MEANDERED	RELUCTANT	REPLENISH	VIGOROUS	REASSURE

Midwife's Apprentice Vocabular

CHRISTENED	DESOLATE	BERATING	INCOMPETENCE	PLUCK
DECEIT	SULLEN	DIRE	RENOWNED	HEEDLESS
TUMULT	THRESHING	FREE SPACE	COMPASSION	GLUTTONY
STANCHING	WRITHING	LUXURIOUS	EXERTIONS	ANTIPODES
RESISTANCE	PATERNOSTERS	TANTALIZING	PROSPEROUS	TWEAKED

Midwife's Apprentice Vocabular

VIGOROUS	TRIUMPHANT	HOIST	IGNORANCE	STUPEFIED
SOOTHSAYERS	HEEDLESS	THRESHING	DISREPUTE	HENCEFORTH
PRIVY	DECEIT	FREE SPACE	TREACHERY	REVELERS
NIMBLE	STOUT	DIRE	CHRISTENED	SUNDRY
COMPASSION	PROSPEROUS	ABBEY	DESOLATE	TUMULT

Midwife's Apprentice Vocabular

SULLEN	RENOWNED	MEANDERED	REASSURE	EFFICACY
WRITHING	INCOMPETENCE	ABUNDANCE	ANTIPODES	BAILIFF
FERMENTING	MEWLING	FREE SPACE	RELUCTANT	LUXURIOUS
WIMPLE	VICTORIOUS	HAGGLING	THRASHED	STANCHING
RESISTANCE	TWEAKED	PATERNOSTERS	TANTALIZING	EXERTIONS

Midwife's Apprentice Vocabular

TRIUMPHANT	TUMULT	RELUCTANT	MEWLING	RESOUNDED
THRASHED	SOLEMNITY	STUPEFIED	INNOVATION	VIGOROUS
ANTIPODES	COMPENDIUM	FREE SPACE	BAILIFF	DIRE
STOUT	GLUTTONY	CHRISTENED	REPLENISH	WIMPLE
TANTALIZING	DESOLATE	HENCEFORTH	HOIST	RENOWNED

Midwife's Apprentice Vocabular

THRESHING	SUNDRY	RESISTANCE	REASSURE	TAUNTED
VICTORIOUS	LUXURIOUS	FERMENTING	TWEAKED	IGNORANCE
PLUCK	PROSPEROUS	FREE SPACE	HEEDLESS	BLIGHT
ABUNDANCE	PRIVY	BERATING	EXERTIONS	MEANDERED
ABBEY	EFFICACY	INCOMPETENCE	PATERNOSTERS	TREACHERY

Midwife's Apprentice Vocabular

BAILIFF	TANTALIZING	INCOMPETENCE	BLIGHT	ABBEY
REVELERS	RESISTANCE	NIMBLE	RENOWNED	HOIST
TUMULT	WIMPLE	FREE SPACE	VIGOROUS	TAUNTED
DIRE	WRITHING	THRESHING	VICTORIOUS	TRIUMPHANT
EFFICACY	TREACHERY	COMPENDIUM	STANCHING	RESOUNDED

Midwife's Apprentice Vocabular

EXERTIONS	HAGGLING	MEANDERED	THRASHED	HEEDLESS
FERMENTING	TWEAKED	INNOVATION	CHRISTENED	ANTIPODES
GLUTTONY	BERATING	FREE SPACE	REPLENISH	LUXURIOUS
PLUCK	RELUCTANT	IGNORANCE	ABUNDANCE	REASSURE
DECEIT	HENCEFORTH	DISREPUTE	SOLEMNITY	SULLEN

Copyrighted

Midwife's Apprentice Vocabular

REASSURE	SOOTHSAYERS	THRESHING	DECEIT	IGNORANCE
PLUCK	VIGOROUS	RENOWNED	HEEDLESS	WRITHING
PATERNOSTERS	HAGGLING	FREE SPACE	DESOLATE	STUPEFIED
INNOVATION	WIMPLE	EXERTIONS	BAILIFF	MEWLING
STANCHING	TWEAKED	INCOMPETENCE	LUXURIOUS	COMPENDIUM

Midwife's Apprentice Vocabular

TREACHERY	TRIUMPHANT	NIMBLE	THRASHED	DIRE
RELUCTANT	TANTALIZING	GLUTTONY	HENCEFORTH	SULLEN
BERATING	EFFICACY	FREE SPACE	FERMENTING	SUNDRY
REVELERS	ANTIPODES	BLIGHT	STOUT	CHRISTENED
COMPASSION	RESISTANCE	REPLENISH	ABUNDANCE	PROSPEROUS

Midwife's Apprentice Vocabular

SUNDRY	WIMPLE	NIMBLE	COMPASSION	CHRISTENED
HEEDLESS	TREACHERY	MEWLING	EXERTIONS	COMPENDIUM
FERMENTING	STUPEFIED	FREE SPACE	LUXURIOUS	TUMULT
EFFICACY	SOOTHSAYERS	THRASHED	REASSURE	INNOVATION
WRITHING	TAUNTED	GLUTTONY	BLIGHT	SULLEN

Midwife's Apprentice Vocabular

TANTALIZING	SOLEMNITY	REPLENISH	DISREPUTE	BAILIFF
TWEAKED	HAGGLING	BERATING	RELUCTANT	TRIUMPHANT
ABBEY	DECEIT	FREE SPACE	IGNORANCE	HENCEFORTH
PATERNOSTERS	INCOMPETENCE	STOUT	REVELERS	RESOUNDED
STANCHING	ANTIPODES	RESISTANCE	VIGOROUS	PLUCK

Midwife's Apprentice Vocabular

REASSURE	WIMPLE	TANTALIZING	STUPEFIED	PROSPEROUS
PLUCK	BERATING	TWEAKED	PRIVY	THRESHING
ANTIPODES	TREACHERY	FREE SPACE	DECEIT	RENOWNED
RELUCTANT	IGNORANCE	LUXURIOUS	CHRISTENED	SUNDRY
HEEDLESS	HOIST	STOUT	DIRE	MEANDERED

Midwife's Apprentice Vocabular

REPLENISH	BLIGHT	VICTORIOUS	EFFICACY	NIMBLE
HENCEFORTH	INCOMPETENCE	RESISTANCE	PATERNOSTERS	RESOUNDED
SOLEMNITY	SULLEN	FREE SPACE	COMPENDIUM	WRITHING
DESOLATE	MEWLING	EXERTIONS	DISREPUTE	GLUTTONY
VIGOROUS	BAILIFF	ABUNDANCE	TRIUMPHANT	COMPASSION

Midwife's Apprentice Vocabular

FERMENTING	BLIGHT	COMPENDIUM	ABBEY	LUXURIOUS
SUNDRY	TRIUMPHANT	HEEDLESS	TANTALIZING	VICTORIOUS
DESOLATE	THRASHED	FREE SPACE	DISREPUTE	ANTIPODES
RENOWNED	SOOTHSAYERS	SULLEN	GLUTTONY	INCOMPETENCE
EFFICACY	RESISTANCE	CHRISTENED	MEANDERED	REASSURE

Midwife's Apprentice Vocabular

RESOUNDED	PRIVY	HENCEFORTH	HAGGLING	PROSPEROUS
STANCHING	RELUCTANT	INNOVATION	WRITHING	STOUT
MEWLING	STUPEFIED	FREE SPACE	EXERTIONS	REVELERS
ABUNDANCE	VIGOROUS	BAILIFF	DIRE	NIMBLE
TWEAKED	WIMPLE	SOLEMNITY	REPLENISH	TREACHERY

Midwife's Apprentice Vocabular

VICTORIOUS	HAGGLING	HOIST	SOLEMNITY	CHRISTENED
DECEIT	WIMPLE	TREACHERY	FERMENTING	BERATING
REASSURE	PLUNK	FREE SPACE	THRASHED	ABBEY
EFFICACY	MEANDERED	ABUNDANCE	IGNORANCE	STANCHING
STOUT	RESISTANCE	REPLENISH	LUXURIOUS	SULLEN

Midwife's Apprentice Vocabular

DESOLATE	PATERNOSTERS	DISREPUTE	TUMULT	DIRE
RELUCTANT	EXERTIONS	TANTALIZING	PROSPEROUS	INCOMPETENCE
REVELERS	NIMBLE	FREE SPACE	BAILIFF	COMPASSION
COMPENDIUM	TWEAKED	HENCEFORTH	RENOWNED	ANTIPODES
SUNDRY	STUPEFIED	THRESHING	INNOVATION	BLIGHT

www.ingramcontent.com/pod-product-compliance
Lightning Source LLC
Chambersburg PA
CBHW081455070526
44586CB00019B/2363